CW01467262

Walking out of the Dark

How I learned to love life again

Kelvyn James

About the Author

Kelvyn James has had many names but settled on this one as it finally felt right. After a bad childhood the first time he can really recall having his own identity, making his own choices, was when he started to rock climb—first in the old dark quarries around Manchester, then the Lake District, Cornwall and North Wales. Eventually this passion took him to the Alps and further afield.

Kelvyn originally funded his climbing with a successful career. Later he started, built and sold a manufacturing business–but those parts of his life seldom carry much measure–it was always the people he shared adventures with that mattered most.

Following a family tragedy in 2010 Kelvyn found himself lost in the dark for many years. As depression took hold, he began to believe the dark was where he deserved to be. But survival skills learned in that abusive childhood, the resilience a life in the outdoors fosters and the good people met along the way all helped him find a way back to loving life again.

Since rebuilding his life Kelvyn has been the Development Officer for the Association of British Climbing Walls, President of the British Association of International Mountain Leaders, a Trustee of Mountain Training and he's the Founder and CEO of Wellness Walks, a charity specialising in supporting people with low mental health to get out into nature. Along the way he's climbed dozens of 4000m peaks in the Alps, led expeditions across the globe, continued to climb esoteric rock routes whenever he can and generally been a big fan of adventuring in many a form. He's also continued to volunteer in mental health support, been a specialist foster carer and picked up a master's degree in psychology.

But he still thinks writing these words may well be the hardest thing he's ever done.

For Catriona who's always been my light,

for the friends who came into the dark to find me,

the special ones who showed me the power of love,

and

for Mum.

Shining bright once more.

First published in 2025 by Wellness Walks

Orton

Penrith

Cumbria

CA10 3RF

www.wellnesswalks.org.uk

ISBN: 978-1-0685194-3-7

Available from:

Amazon.co.uk

Signed copies:
wellnesswalks.org.uk

Words from after, to be read before

The last decade and more has been a journey of discovery and recovery. Of slowly finding my own understanding of many a thing. Then the process of bringing them into the light; figuring out how to say them aloud, to acknowledge them, own them. At times the words that follow have seemed to have a life of their own, have emerged raw needing to be shaped, or arrived angry and belligerent, refusing to change. I just hope they're at least readable, maybe make sense, and I really do hope you can follow my flow. But ultimately these are my chosen words alone; that's just how they are and how they need to be, for me.

Because I've never really been a fan of rules of literature, life or love that seem to serve no purpose. The imposition of someone else's beliefs, views or quirks somehow deemed more important than those of others. So right here, even before the old words start to appear on the pages to come, I'm going to break the biggest rule in the writing of a book – I'm going to tell you the ending.

I'm telling you now that parts of the beginning—or rather, the place this story starts from—are full of sorrow, horror and pain. And whilst they're vital to any understanding of the how and the why, they're not the whole of the story and I hope they're not what you carry forward with you when we're done.

Because this story has a happy ending.

I want you to know that now so that when it seems like we're lost in the dark, you'll have that knowledge to guide you on.

Contents

Words from after, to be read before   7

Introduction: my truth   9

1. Falling   11

2. Son of a Murdered Mum   29

3. Time Travelling   53

4. Voices in the Dark   67

5. Learning to Fly   85

6. My Son the Mountaineer   101

7. Remember me with a Smile   123

8. Shining Stars   143

9. Wandering in Wonder   169

10. Acceptance; Resting in Peace   187

Epilogue; Endings   201

Words of a new beginning   205

Introduction: my truth

If someone carries a great weight for too long one of two things will happen; either they will break, or they will get stronger.

For the longest time I didn't know which it would be.

In 2010 my mother was brutally murdered by her husband and my world was shattered into pieces I thought could never be woven together again. That world, my own little world in which I believed I'd finally found my place, ceased to exist.

As I wrote the word 'world' there, I almost changed it to 'life' – but of course, 'life' goes on. Inexplicably, inextricably the seconds and minutes, the hours and days, they all continue to tick by whilst you remain locked fast in a moment you can never escape. Other people pass by without really seeing you, and as your world gets darker you become too afraid to reach out for fear of pulling them down with you. I'd thought myself strong, secure, a survivor. But, even if I didn't know it at the time, in the space of four words I began a fall into the abyss that would last years:

"Your Mum's been murdered."

There'd have been a dozen and more kind, comforting and heartfelt words wrapped around that terrible news. But they are, and forever will be, just a few of the many things lost that day.

Some moments carry so much consequence that they fracture time, they cast a dark shadow into both the past and the future, one that redefines everything.

It took a long while to be able to coax into existence the words I've written. Longer still to acknowledge what they collectively say, and a decade gone before I could even begin to think about others ever seeing them, seeing what they said of me.

It's been the toughest fight of my life to reach a point where there's enough light to be able to open the box of regrets I wrapped in chains of anger and hate and buried at the bottom of my broken heart. The words written here might well be my truth. They may have changed, from their beginning to their end. And yet, however they fall forth, these are the words I hope may eventually show me a way out of the dark.

I think I need to tell you that I wrote this for an audience of one. An audience that has taken some hard knocks and gotten back up, an audience that has spent a long time looking into that abyss, has possibly gotten too comfortable with the horrors that look back. Any truth within these words is mine alone, they speak for no-one else. It's my truth seen through my own glass, darkly. It's never anyone's place to speak the words of other people's lives, I can only share my own why and how of getting to here. But, and there'll be a lot of buts…

…if a single reader can take a solitary ounce of comfort from the path I've walked, if I can light just one candle for just one person, then the darkness is less than it was. That counts as a win.

Parts of what follows are hard to read and I apologise. I've possibly gotten too used to the saying of terrible things, it's quite possible they should be shouted more and just as possible I shouldn't apologise.

There'll be a lot of contradictions too.

If someone carries a great weight for too long one of two things will happen; either they will break, or they will get stronger.

I'm beginning to understand it might well be both.

Chapter 1

Falling

I

It's January 2010 and my mum is violently stabbed to death in her own home by her third husband.

I've tried to make that sentence as simple as possible because every single word of it fails to come close to conveying the horror of what happened that day, and yet their collective impact has shaped every moment since, shaded every moment before.

It's 1974 and I'm flying through the air, an infant thrown violently against a wall by an angry grown man.

I've tried to make that sentence as simple as possible because every single word of it fails to come close to conveying what my childhood was like, and yet their collective impact says nearly everything about my path to today.

The realisation that the two are so interconnected has been one of the hardest revelations of my life. The realisation that the two are so interconnected is so profoundly obvious that I'm staggered I could be so blind to it for so long. In coming to an understanding of the how, the why and the what that brought me to here I've come close to being lost for good. And yet, somehow, I've managed to find a way to remake myself whole again. Forever scarred, never to be all of who I once was but, I hope, maybe stronger, maybe, just maybe, something more than before.

Everything is now irrevocably altered by that one terrible moment which I've gradually come to realise was the turning point of a life that had been touched by both joy and sorrow until then. I thought I'd left behind the shadows of an unhappy youth, I thought I was thriving out in the light, living my latter life well. I never imagined I could fall again. I believed that the fear, anger, pain and self-loathing were all things vanquished and gone. Wrapped in my own little world I still thought the past was a fixed thing, done; that the simple passing of time had moved me further and further away from the dark days of before.

We'd all have spoken to Mum a fair bit over that Christmas holiday season—I may even have seen her, I'm sure I, we, would have—but subsequent events so eviscerated the time around then that I can't honestly recall now with any kind of clarity or certainty. Another thing lost, another of the holes in my mind that will come to shape the next decade, that will come to redefine all of the ones before.

So where to start? Now, as then, it's all so entwined, distance has both distorted and distilled, made some connections seem obvious, stolen the sense of others. I now know there were days, years, a lifetime smouldering up to that fatal moment. I also know that in that one act of evil she was gone and I began a long fall down into the dark. So, I can only ever start from there.

Somehow I need to find a way to tell you the where, the how and the why of the incomprehensible.

One wet, shitty, nondescript night at the turn of the last decade, in a wet, shitty, nondescript seaside town my mother came home to her death at the hands of the wet, shitty, nondescript man, she loved. It'll take forever and longer to fathom any understanding of how and why life ever got to that cataclysmic moment — as long again to find an acceptance of the part I played in letting it happen.

Sat typing this many lifetimes later I can see myself then, and now circling, avoiding, knowing I'm dancing around the edge of the abyss—knowing that to ever move towards a sense of forward, there needs to be some version of events to pick apart and reassemble. I know that in trying to bring forth the words I hope can guide me back into the light, I'll have to turn back into the dark, to look again at things no one should ever experience, to write down words that will undoubtedly cause pain and anguish, that will threaten as much as they answer.

My mother's murderer has never offered any truthful or even sane version, leaving her ending a mass of unanswered questions, unknown horrors, regret laid bare. Any truth, if indeed any can even be found, will be mine alone. Others may well see events unfold from a different point of view, their tangential perspective giving them their own unique interpretation, but I can only try to put into words my version of a truth. And only hope that in doing so it helps me find a way to salve my soul.

At the turn of the last decade my mother came back from a normal Friday at work and found the door locked from the inside, her keys useless, no answer coming from within. It must have seemed just another unwelcome twist in the crumbling catastrophe her marriage had become. Why she didn't just leave, why she didn't call any of us then will be just the first of many questions to haunt me evermore, but instead she called a local friend. He broke the door open, and then, in a moment I hope haunts him for ever and longer, he left her to enter alone. Not a single neighbour opened their own door to check at the sounds of splintering wood, to offer shelter or a simple kind word. Perhaps they were too used to it by then, perhaps they just didn't care. My mother walked through that shattered door and never walked out again.

What followed happened for reasons we can never really know. Her third husband, the man she still loved, the man she thought she was rebuilding her life with, the man we'd all tolerated for so long, tolerated for her sake, that man attacked her in a drunken rage with a kitchen knife.

But... the first of so many exceptional grammatical pauses... moments when the words struggle to form in the realisation of their weight...that doesn't come close to the reality of what happened that night. Words, however hard I try, will never be enough to describe what he did to my mum. In a frenzied attack that must have lasted an amount of time both too short to comprehend and too long to endure he stabbed her again and again and again and again. The coroner listed in excess of one hundred different wounds and recorded that any one of a dozen of them would have been fatal, the savagery of his attack making it impossible to tell which finally stole her life. The media have normalised words like frenzy, and savagery, and attack through overuse. Murder and loss are now the staple fare of Sunday night entertainment. Coroners do no such thing. Every word is chosen precisely. With the precision of a knife wound.

My mother fought for her life. Defensive wounds that made her hands unrecognisable gave testament to how she desperately tried, in vain, to hold him off, how valiantly she fought to survive, how hard she tried to escape, how utterly relentless his attack was. He stabbed her again and again. Worse, if that's bearable, was to come.

And I need to say here: her murderer changed his story each time a new vanity arose in his head. No truth has ever come from him. Yet the coroner and the police never once wavered in the statement of fact without reason. The evidence painted a picture too awful to acknowledge, too horrific to deny. He stabbed Mum again and again and again; every major organ damaged, bones broken by his blade, her blood let loose everywhere. The patterns in that blood making it cruelly clear she was alive for so much of it until eventually she must have fallen to the floor unable to withstand his onslaught. And he kept stabbing her. The coroner told the court that her wounds indicated that he continued to stab her long after life had left her body. My mum lay dead at his feet on the floor of the home they bought together. And he stabbed her over and over again. He did the same to her the next day. And the day after that. He spent three days mutilating Mum, desecrating whatever was left of her.

This pathetic little man, someone who'd spent years progressing from odd to annoying, from strange to unpleasant, from forgettable to forgotten. We'd never noticed he'd moved from verbal to violent, from controlling to uncontrolled, from man to monster. As he slowly empowered himself by driving a wedge between Mum and her friends, made her family not want him (and thus them) around, he trapped her in a place none of us could see, trapped her somehow in plain sight, yet lost. I thought he was just a nothing, and in doing so I failed to stop him taking everything.

He stabbed her so many times. He took her life and then when there seemed nothing left to take he took her dignity. Mum lay dead on the living room floor and yet he still found ways to hurt what was left of her. That was how he spent those three terrible days. It defies understanding but at various points over that weekend, as we were later to see on CCTV evidence at his trial, he left the apartment to go and buy more alcohol. He must have had to literally scrub my mother's blood from his skin to be able to go out and feed his craven craving. With blood red footprints leaving a trail from lounge to hallway to door, he walked out into the day like he hadn't a care in the world. Over the course of that weekend he lied to concerned friends when they called. He bought his booze and chatted to the shop staff, he even spoke to my maternal Grandfather on the phone, Mum lying there dead on the floor, her lifeblood slowly drying in the tattered carpet. He concocted a litany of lies to tell a worried old man about his first-born daughter. Did he even glance over his shoulder at Mum's cold corpse? Did the reality of his actions before him on the floor mean a thing? He acted like they were any of the other sorry days of his sad little life. He was busy on the internet buying and selling memorabilia. He fed himself and he drank more and more. And then he stabbed her, dead though she was. Still he stabbed her where she lay fallen, thankfully now gone.

One of the many things he never did was show any remorse or decency, something that won't change however many words I write. At the trial other details will emerge, it will be a crucible of sorrows, but we'll never know the 'why' of what happened that terrible night, other than the tragedy the police pieced together from the evidence. Later I'll spend years stuck in dreadful dialogue with this worst of all people, but I'll never know any more about why than I did then or now.

And where was I? At home sixty miles away, doing whatever fools do just before their world stops spinning. I'll have been wrapped up in the inconsequential moments of my own existence. Whatever I thought might have mattered at the time is now another trivial detail thankfully lost, one less shame to remember.

I'll have been irritated at Mum's latest drama with the shitty little man because I knew she was missing. I knew she hadn't met up with my grandfather as planned. But I didn't do a thing. I'll have been annoyed that she's even with the shitty little man because I know he's hit her before, and she stayed. He assaulted her drunk, not the first man to hit her, but one who I should have stopped. He hit her, and just as every abuser does at first, he told her it was a mistake, that he loved her, that he needed her, that it wasn't his fault, and she stayed. And I was so angry. I was angry at him, but fool that I am, I was angrier at her for staying. And I did nothing. All that apparent power, all that love, and I did nothing. I didn't make him leave. I didn't even make him think about consequences. I didn't have a couple of blokes put him in one of our vans so we could have a less than friendly chat. I didn't tell her to leave. I didn't let her know she could always tell me anything. I didn't tell her I'd keep her safe. I didn't protect her as a son should. A shame that will damn me forever.

Because that's the last time she'll ever tell you.

She never tells anyone he's hit her again.

That's how domestic violence works. You get one chance. If you're lucky. One chance to do the right thing.

She'll never tell you so many things again now. She bites her lip and takes it when he drags her by her hair, threatens her in public, bites her.

At the trial we'll discover he's on bail for assaulting her when he takes her life, that he chased her into the village police station and lifted her off her feet by her throat while hitting her in the head. He chose to punch her in the head because she'd not long had brain surgery. At that moment, like all the others, he knows exactly what he's doing. He knows she's not going anywhere. He's not even scared of me, why would he be? I've not done anything about it. I've let this happen. The police pull him off, charge him against Mum's wishes. They don't tell me. They don't tell anyone. They shouldn't have to; I should have known. I've been none of the things a son should be. I'm falling already and I don't even know it. I deserve the coming darkness. I deserve how much this will hurt.

I think I'm sat in the upstairs window, maybe there's a scotch in my hand. Maybe I'm snoozing in the afternoon sun, maybe I'm throwing a ball with a beautiful white dog. I'm content. In a world that I'm already falling out of, the abyss about to open beneath my feet, and I'll not even have noticed the dark shadow of what was to come. I won't have felt my grasp on that world start to give. Despite so many previous falls, I'll have missed the moment that's going to redefine everything. I won't have had a clue that I'm weightless in the between, neither before and not yet after. It'll take me a long time to be able to look back and realise all those earlier falls may just help me to survive the one about to come.

II

Because I've fallen before – in a less metaphorical sense – fallen in the way that gravity intends, the way that ends with a sudden sharp stop. A lifetime of climbing, cragging, hitting big hills; I thought I knew. I thought I was a survivor. One second everything's on the line, gripped, balanced, moving inch by inch upward with care and then: a second of weightless disbelief, watching gear rip, tiny hopeful pauses each time they nearly catch you, the ground rushing up to meet you with a bone s splintering impact. Foolish games. If you play long enough you'll fall in the end.

An old climber once said "if you're not falling you're not trying hard enough," and I know what he meant. But my mindset always veered more towards "if you're trying hard enough, you shouldn't fall". If you climb nowadays though, falling is all a part of the game. Steep climbing walls with bolted protection make it almost fun – and that's what most new climbers know.

But. Everything has a but.

Climbing outdoors adds so many variables. Sure, there are bolt—protected routes outdoors; on the continent they're the norm, but not in the UK. Here most climbing is protected with temporary gear placed into natural weaknesses – and so the variabilities increase by a multitude, much like life. Now you have the rock itself to consider, other people, the frequency (or not) with which you can find places to put protection, your skill in placing gear, how much gear you can afford, how much you can carry, your judgement, your fitness—the list goes on and on, the variables multiplying exponentially like the days of our lives. Take yourself into the big mountains and you multiply it all by scale and consequence. Here the age—old adage of the leader must not fall still feels true… but. Everyone falls.

The greatest rock climber of my generation once told me that there's a magic moment to be found at the crux point of a difficult move: the moment where you're truly weightless, where momentum counters gravity, where intent meets purpose. For non—climbers I'd guess it's the moment your stomach lifts as the rollercoaster tips from climb to plummet and you hang free for a split second, weightless and feeling ready to fly.

I think we can find that moment before any fall.

When you're out there on the edge and your grip falters. When your sinews flex, toes lift to try and push you up, hips twist you inward, there's a moment. Not the moment you might be thinking of, that comes an instant later. No, there's a moment when you are both things at once – climber and fallen, you've won and lost, right then you are both before and after. Weightless-in-waiting, gravity's grip about to rush you to the ground. There's a moment of hope. Time pauses, you think you can still latch on, make contact, fight the inevitable. And in that moment, are you falling, fallen or flying? It's a moment I thought I knew, synapses firing, endorphins flooding the system, disbelief on pause, a tiny insignificance in the inevitability of what comes next.

Invincibility – it's a common illusion of youth – one I most certainly had out there on the rock face. I knew I was good. I'd surfed that moment so many times – and without fail I'd catch on when it mattered most, take hold, breathe and *be*. I could rationalise the risks. I took positive action to mitigate them. But that invincible part of me knew they didn't really apply to me. I'd survived my abusive past, I could survive anything.

But. We all fall eventually.

Surviving so many times I thought I knew the rules, the tricks, how to play the odds. You might imagine it happens so fast that there's little to tell, but time is an elusive concept at best. It doesn't follow rules, and we have only the most limited understanding of our own capabilities within time's flow. I think we have no real understanding of the interaction between the two. I could tell you the most amazing details from inside those moments. The exact sound a rope makes as it tightens, contracts and then releases. The patination of the rock where the sweat from my fingertips still glistens in beads too small to see but large enough to slide me away. The surge of adrenaline as it rushes through my blood. All things happening at a rate too fast to fathom, happening ahead and outside of our comprehension. And yet, not a fraction of the whole. Because in that instant, when your everything should be solely focused into the now – other thoughts, memories and ghosts arrive, clear as day. I've held the ropes whilst others have fallen. Observed from the outside as it happens in a blur of fast forward motion, impossible for the watcher to take in any conscious detail. Perhaps time is working differently for those on different ends of the rope.

Yet did I really know the odds? Had I mastered the game? The house always wins, the Devil wants his due—and now I'm smiling a hard learned, rueful smile. You can't practice consequences.

Because then I fell in the most physical way. Just like you thought I would.

Showing off, feeling on top of my game, telling my climbing partner "I'll show you how it's done." All the little rituals gone in a moment's rashness, high on the wall before I've even really thought about the route. And now I've properly fucked up. I know it, I can sense through the rope my partner knows it too. I'm comfortable right here but I can't make the next move with any belief and I haven't a hope of down-climbing the moves I've just done to get fast to here. That's not good. I can try go with my left... but the crack slopes the other way... I know I'll not be able to hold it... tentatively I try, I begin to move. My right foot is stood on something the size of an old half pence piece with all my weight. My left is high on a matchstick—wide ledge, but with my knee much higher than my hip there's no weight on it... that's the hope of what might be. As I try to turn my hips to raise my shoulders my weighted foot slips and I have to reverse myself quickly. A pause, deep breaths, rebalance. I reach up and out far left. I'm strong but not that strong. Finger tendons scream. And then I do it – I look down at my last runner. It's only a few feet beneath me, two more runners in the crack lower down. I already knew all of that, why did I look? Now I've acknowledged the unseen weight of consequences. Now I'm considering how comprehensive my insurance policy really is. The fear is building, I can taste it.

But. I still believe I've got this. I lower myself back down so all my weight is on that tiny fraction of friction. The wall is vertical, my hands are out wide, but it's a rest of sorts. I breathe, heart rate lowers. I've got this. I've got power to spare. I know I need to crossover and lead with my right hand, swivel my weight up and onto my left foot. I know I've wrong-handed myself, it's not knowledge that helps right now though, it's just extra weight. Statically that next hold is a good two feet past my maximum reach with my right hand. I lean back, thought becoming action before senses can complain. Dynamically I bounce down and launch up and across. Hips and shoulders turning together. My weight lifts off my right foot as I rise. My proprioceptive movement is good, even unseen my right index and centre fingertips hit the crack at the sweet spot. My thumb locks them onto the crack's edge as my left knee straightens. I'm there, this is the moment Johnny will try to explain decades later, weightless, full of opportunity.

And then I'm not. I'm off. In throwing my weight. My fragile relationship with that thin left foothold has failed—two fingertips can balance, but cannot hold my weight.

Time pauses. I'm gone in the space of a tick, future me knows that by tock I'll be a heap of bloody broken bones on the ground below. But in that gap between cause and effect I'm relaxed; I can remember the rush, angry at myself, tensing and turning my face away from the rock. Knowing as the gear takes my weight I'll slam into the crag with a crash. Then the gear rips free of the crack. Time slows even further; I'm still falling inside that first tick. Then as now I think "this will hurt". I'm now going to hit the second runner hard. Subconsciously I've done the one thing those who want to survive shouldn't really do: I've braced for impact. And it doesn't come. There's the slightest of pauses as this gear also considers any idea it might have had about catching me – then it rips too. I'm out of time, tick has slammed into tock. And I don't have the time left to realise just how much this is really going to hurt.

So many falls, all connected in so many ways.

When you live what most would describe as an adventurous life, when your chosen happiness has been labelled extreme, when you go to the places others don't, there are certain questions you'll always get asked. One that turns up with predictable frequency is:

"What's the worst thing that's ever happened to you?"

Now for a long time I would never have acknowledged to strangers, friends, hell pretty much anyone including myself, the abuse of my childhood, and for certain the answer I'd give you would have been "falling off a cliff in the Peak District and breaking my legs. Feeling my heels drive through my ankle joints.

Knowing my tibias and fibulas had broken, ripping the ligaments to shreds, too scared to move enough to find out if I've broken my neck" and for most enquirers that would be a gruesome enough vindication that their life of comfort was a preferable choice to venturing forth into the wilderness. Climbers, of course, would laugh and tell me I should have held on. They're both right. There's nothing wrong with comfortable. However we fall, we all hold on until we can't any longer.

So many factors that day: not being where I should, thankfully being where I was. The RAF mountain rescue team on a training exercise who came to assist. A hospital long since closed that took me in. The junior doctor, also a climber. A consultant prepared to forgo the easy surgical fix of crippling me, to wait and give me a chance. Discovering the pain threshold to be able to withstand trial electrical therapy. I spent two weeks in hospital. My boss visited me every day, my family not once. I lied to the girlfriend who'd later become my wife, just to get her through graduation; I'm embarrassed by that still. I was in a wheelchair for a month, crutches for two more. We're not invincible in our youth, but we are elastic. Twelve months later I tied on to a rope. Paid attention to each and every move. Got my hands right. Finished the climb.

III

Back then I still thought of time as a linear journey, and as I left moments lost in my past I thought they were forever gone.

Fool.

This, like so much of the before, will come back to haunt me.

Two and a half decades later, just as I'm just starting to think I can see some light after the horror of losing Mum, I slip on a path. I'm doing nothing more strenuous than walking up to a high camp somewhere in the UK's Lake District. Somewhere unglamorous and unknown – some obscure contour feature near High Street. I fall with a full rucksack on my back on yet another awful stone highway path and land crumpled on the ground. I swear profusely in the forlorn hope that profanity will somehow fix it. It seldom does. I sit there and feel sorry for myself for a while then eventually I start to move. It hurts, but I'm used to pain. We've all gone over on an ankle. I make camp and mentally abandon my plans to go climbing by moonlight. The next day it's swollen and black. I strap it up, break camp and half crawl home. I'll walk it off.

I don't. It takes two years to get a proper diagnosis, and during those years I follow all the well-intentioned physio's advice to keep moving, to push on. I become exceptionally adept at gritting my teeth. I later learn I've effectively been walking on a broken ankle for two years which caused a shard of bone from that original accident to become dislodged and slowly grind like a drill through my ankle joint. The first two surgeons only ever look at my x-rays and MRI scans—neither bother with the CT scans as they've found an apparently easy explanation. They haven't. Both want to fuse the joint and cripple me, leave me hobbling, but pain free, with a stick for the rest of my life. It takes another year to find a surgeon capable of something possibly better. A good kind man who looks me in the eye and tells me just what my odds[1] are; puts a hand on my shoulder and explains I'll probably never climb again. I might still walk with a stick. He tells me the secret of recovery will ultimately lie within me. I trust him and that's a rare and special thing, considering I'm only just learning to trust me again. I sign the consent form. Twelve months after surgery, I'm finally able to walk and work again.

Those lost years of pain are another long hard fall back into the abyss. Self-doubt, fuelled by recrimination and regret, make me

---

[1] Mr P reckoned I'd a 25% chance the operation would still result in me needing the bones to be fused. There was a 10% chance I'd make a 100% recovery and the odds were I'd land somewhere in between. He also told me he only took me on as he'd never operated on a mountaineer before.

begin to believe I deserve to lose the everything I have left, that I couldn't possibly deserve the chance of happiness, that I owe the universe too large a debt. I thought I knew about falling. I thought I was strong enough to climb back up. The dark had other ideas. There's a price to pay, and this time you might not have enough left. Deep in the abyss something barks a bitter laugh; I think it's my destiny.

"What's the worst thing that's ever happened to you?"

Later in life I could, and often did, avoid a truthful answer with a painful anecdote. Waking to see a worried surgeon and his anaesthesiologist with your wife at your bedside, to hear the words "we thought we'd lost you there for a second" over some unknown near-miss while I was under, the ghost of tears in your love's eyes... that takes some getting your head around. But of course the pain of those you love is always far worse than your own. Seeing loved ones go far too soon, watching them disappear to insidious conditions we should have a cure for by now, sitting holding the hand of someone you love who no longer knows your name.

And I've known people suffer far worse physical torment than me. The ones that didn't walk again. The friends fallen on the mountain never to come home. The friends fallen on the mountain and never found.

But.

I'd first fallen long ago even if it'll never be long enough to forget. Does it count as falling if you're knocked down or thrown? Yes it does. In the worst possible way.

I'll write about my childhood later—about how the pattern was set before I even knew the words, about how all those years ago helped make the path to now, then and everything betwixt possible. But.

The thing I now choose to remember most from that dark childhood isn't the falling, it's the getting back up. It hurt more if you were on the ground. He won if you didn't get up. Standing up and gritting your teeth would get you hit again, knocked down again. But it meant you'd won, just for a moment, the smallest of wins. Even if you had to hide that little victory deep down inside you, not let it loose in the world. Even then I was building strong little boxes.

And of course, many a time, most times in fact, you simply lay there, beaten again.

Getting back up when you carry the weight of being told you're worthless is nearly impossible. Most people have someone to help – a parent, maybe a mum – but what if they're also scared, cowered, and broken? What if you're just a child and you can't see or understand that? Then you're on your own.

Getting back up is the most difficult thing in the world.

There's a term I've come to learn in this latter life as I've fought to find my way to here: *emotional resilience*. It means, whatever the psychologists might tell you[2], getting back up. I didn't know it then but those first early falls, whatever other damage they undoubtedly did, they may well have been the thing that gave me the strength to survive what was to come.

"What's the worst thing that's ever happened to you?"

Everything is redefined now. Everything I thought I knew gone in an instant. Moments burn with a furnaced intensity, searing the back of my eyes when I close then, smouldering through the dark hours when I cannot sleep. Any benchmark that I thought I had,

---

[2] Edith Grotberg defines resilience as the human capacity to deal with, overcome, learn from or even be transformed by challenges in life.

that I thought I could comprehend—any measure of "worst" I thought I knew—none of them register anymore.

And of course, they do. Pain still flares along nerves and I feel sorry for myself. I occasionally wince as I walk and I question the choices I've made. I face more surgery and I ponder why I have to push so hard? And there are still days when the glowering red box buried at the heart of it all pulls me back towards the abyss. Then I remember. I pause, I centre, I reconnect. I've learned to catch myself in that moment of self-pity. That moment, when for the briefest of illusions, I'm weightless again, paused. That moment just before reality hits home and I remember what the worst things to ever happen really are. Because when I close my eyes it isn't my climbing accidents, the dark days of childhood or any other petty sorrows that haunt my dreams. All those things make the abyss deeper, but they're not the real horror that lies waiting in the darkest depths.

"What's the worst thing that's ever happened to you?"

Standing broken in a forlorn apartment looking at the Rorschach red outline of your mother's last moments stained forever into a threadbare carpet.

Seeing the pattern of blood droplets across the walls where a knife swung again and again has thrown them. Seeing that pattern even when you close your eyes.

The smell of the police's forensic site cleaning agent. A smell not strong enough to completely mask the stench of your failure.

Finding a hidden box of pictures from your childhood that she'd kept safe down the decades, knowing we were never strong enough to talk of it when we were together.

Standing in a dock and being questioned by your mother's murderer about how much you loved her. How you didn't love her enough.

Realising you would kill a man if you could.

Knowing you can't stop the tears of the ones you love.

Reaching for the phone to make a call that can never be answered.

Knowing that you could have done more.

Knowing that you should have done more.

Hating yourself for not doing more.

Hating yourself for still being here.

There are so, so, so many worse things than most people ever imagine.

Chapter 2

Son of a murdered mum

I

I am the son of a murdered mum.

These are harsh words, cruel words, but ultimately, sadly, they are true words. They are words that no-one should ever have to say or hear, yet now they are the words that whisper to me in the dark, words that threaten to consume me, words I cannot escape. They are words that I fear will come to define me. It's the truth of who I now am.

I am the son of a murdered mum. It is difficult to put a reality to these words. I've said them aloud, to myself, my loved ones, to groups of strangers—but the meaning of them bears little examination, to dwell on these words is to slowly prise at the bonds that keep you sane, to pick over the scab that tries to form on a wound that will never heal. They crept up on me, in the midst of my anger and grief, words written by a tabloid editor, a phrase that slowly took hold with a grip I couldn't shake, a refrain that echoed as I lay in bed, that jolted around my head as I ran. Slowly but surely these words began to change me. At first it was a slow incipient change, eventually it was a physical change, but always it was a painful change, a loss of self, a metamorphosis into someone no-one would want to be.

I am a son.

I have a mum. Had, not have, never again to hold.

Because she was murdered.

Each word true, a simple statement of fact.

Each word a vivid scar on what little is left of my soul. The weight of these words holds me down in the dark. Each word the echo of a damnation I feel I deserve.

There's an old magic in names, a power of knowledge in the naming of a thing. In many a mythology to know the true name of someone proffers power over them. I was born Kelvyn Blomfield yet I never knew that name. My teenage mother's first husband, my genetic father, was a shallow excuse of a man who abandoned his teenage bride and the two tiny children he'd never acknowledge before I was even able to talk. No great loss there. I was made a Humphries by my mother's marriage to a cruel and nasty man, her second husband, my stepfather, but it was never my name, rather one I carried like a crown of thorns, a never-true thing that never felt right. Completing the sad history of the terrible men my mother loved, Stephen Green, her third husband and the one who killed her, though all three most surely played their part in how it ever got to that, a name I'd eradicate forever if I could. But. There is a power in names.

When we buried Mum we couldn't bring ourselves to put any of those unworthy names on her grave; it'll forever read "Carole, much loved daughter, sister, mother, grandmother and friend" and I've made my peace with that. When I married I knew I still carried a name that deserved to disappear and so I chose a new family name. One that rang true. An old name from the early years, a name I remembered that wrapped me in love—I hoped it would be a truth that would lift me up.

So is it the naming of a thing that makes it so? We all create our own autobiographical self and at the same time are defined by others; often with no conscious thought as to the process of it all. The more balanced of us can marry the two together. Before, I had been Kelvyn, or Husband, or Friend, or Boss. I was a climber, I had aspirations to be a mountaineer. A good guy or a bad guy—I could be any and all of these, and at first, after, I thought I still was. But as the terrible words took hold, as they made their dominion known, the other names fell away and other people began, I was sure, to define me by the terrible words instead. I'd hear them whispered as voices dropped away when I entered a room. Their presence hung in the air, merciless reminders of my horror and shame, in the long dark hours they'd come and tap—tap—tap at my sense of self like Poe's callous raven. But worse, obviously worse, slowly I began to redefine myself by them. As I strove to move on, albeit forever changed, as I came to realise I was held fast, that I was falling out of love with life… it was then that the words really began to exert the power they held. It was then that I began to frame myself and my life within the prison of that terrible phrase.

A decade later I find myself stood in front of a group of outdoor instructors delivering a First Aid for Mental Health course; module 2 deals with stigma. Do we stigmatise the victims of domestic violence? Most definitely. Do the victims stigmatise themselves? Without question. But what about the survivors—the ones left picking up the pieces? It's painfully easy to now see how quickly, how deeply I wrapped myself in that shroud of shame, one all of my own making, even to this day its tattered remains cling to my psyche. Looking back through years of journal entries I find repeated use of phrases like "on these days when I deserve to hurt," "one day I might make a peace with what I didn't do," "an absolution I'll never receive." As I tell the class that stigma is a pathway to self-loathing, self-harm and worse—how it reinforces negative perceptions, deepens depression, it's impossible not to make my own internal connections to behaviours, decisions, scars. There, laid bare, another of the many paths I've wandered lost to here.

It's not a thing you're conscious of. As the life you once had slowly slips away there's no sense of loss, the change isn't writ large enough to notice. Well, not at first. I didn't wake one morning and decide this would be my new identity, I doubt I was even aware it was happening until it was too late. Did I say the actual words out loud? I'm sure I did, but the real change was in my perception of reality. Gradually little else continued to matter. I lurched from one focal point to another: Green being charged, waiting for a trial date, waiting for the coroner to release Mum, the funeral, then the longer wait for the trial. Running, hurting, pushing further to hurt more. Ostensibly some things were constructive, but they were diversions; Fundraising for Women's Aid, writing Just Giving pages and articles, speaking at events. All seem good, look positive, feel like they should be steps in the 'moving on' that everybody tells you to aim for. But they all had a common theme: they all revolved around that black hole at the centre of everything, locked me fast in the inescapable gravity of a moment in time. All were genuinely intended to be helpful but a decade later I'm now not so sure—they all stopped any real form of grieving and kept me falling away from the light.

II

When I realised that the papers had the story, as it became clear that they'd run with it, I just instinctively knew that I wanted everyone to hear it first from me. However impossible that was, it seemed in that instant the most important thing I could do. Grief-blind I sat down at a computer, selected 'All' in the contacts field and began to write an email. I'd no idea what to say, I can't recollect what I wrote and I'm not sure I any longer want to know, but eventually I hit send. Almost immediately my phone rang, a friend calling from France to tell me he thought I must have been hacked as he'd just received the most awful email that had apparently gone to over 500 people. As he paused in the flow of his upset and concern I had to tell him the words were mine and what they said was true. Then I just hung up. I couldn't process other people.

I can remember the first friendly journalist who contacted us via the fundraising page. The well-practiced concern, the way she smoothly slid past the defences me, myself and I thought we'd put in place. How she weaselled her way past friends and family, the slow knife that cuts to the core. How earnestly she wanted to do a supportive piece about the horrors of domestic violence. She was affable, on our side, thought mum's story could help other women. At least she was, right up until I said I didn't think it was the right time; I don't even think I said no. And suddenly the veneer vanished; how quickly her 'supportive' slithered through 'sensationalist' and arrived at 'sickening'. Then the phrase I've come to understand explains the UK's populist press: "if you don't speak to me I'll just write it anyway". A poisoned paradox. I felt damned if I didn't and so there it was, in bright bold print "Son of Murdered Mum speaks out". The die was cast and my shade crept out into the world. I was damned when I did.

We all said no to press more than once, twice or even thrice. And yes we also did do some. My brother had friends at ITV, they were amazingly kind and listened, they reported on the fundraising, focused on finding something positive to build from tragedy; but they were the exception. My business had a relationship, or so I thought, with our local newspaper. But there it was one cold wet Thursday in January. They'd called asking for a comment or a quote; I'd said no. I'd explained I didn't want to walk the streets of Kendal with people pointing and looking. I made it clear I thought they owed me more than that. They clearly didn't think they did, or maybe all the money we spent on advertising with them really meant less than I thought but there it was that Thursday morning: "Local Man's Mum Murdered." The words didn't need to be exactly the same, but their effect was, another crack in my sense of self, our little hometown no longer a refuge.

And of course this was happening in the emerging reach of social media. A decade later I'm sat in front of a screen a little wiser and the tide seems to be turning, we're starting to acknowledge the hostile effects of keyboard warriors and the sad little people who create their fake profiles, but back then we really did think it was a community of friends. One of many harshly won life lessons; it wasn't. People I couldn't have named from a seaside town I'd done everything to forget all had an opinion. Speculation was rife, a lot of it was vile, most of it was hurtful, little was well meant. And of course many people simply disappeared, the friends who were never friends. And I know the reality was some people were stars in a firmament of darkness, but more of that later. At this moment in time's complex swirl I'm too far into the abyss to realise the worth of those shining stars.

Slowly, burning deeper and deeper each time, the terrible words seared their way into my soul.

For a while I tried to embrace them, there was a sense of honouring mum in acknowledging them. Could, or indeed should, any other role ever be more important? Everything else was simply banal in comparison, I felt shallow and disloyal when I thought of those other versions of myself, of the other roles I should have been living. I can't say with any certainty that I thought of life beyond the next milestone—and every milestone was intrinsically linked to Mum.

I can rationalise that four of us went on holiday days after we finally buried Mum, but I can't tell you a thing about the trip. I know we continued to run the business—as the UK's recession tightened I know that we were making major changes, restructuring, moving into new sectors—I just can't remember any of the how, when or where. Looking back now I can only credit that to Cat, my wife, holding me, us and our business together.

III

There's a process to grief; psychologists refer to the Kubler-Ross Grief Cycle, people apparently wiser than at least me have tried to put bereavement and loss into little boxes. I like boxes, god knows I've spent a lifetime trying to keep them buried and bound—but the hard lesson of time is they never stay locked, they always leak out into the world. Perhaps wisdom will one day show me that's a blessing too.

Denial. Theoretically I know this happened, that there was a point in the telling when the self simply couldn't process what it was hearing—but in truth I think I knew the moment Cat came through to tell me there was a call I had to take. We'd known Mum was missing, but we'd never have consciously thought this. So many connections you don't see till it's far too late. The spike of emotion, the sensory overload masks it, but I can accept it was there. But a few hours later I see it play out on the face of someone I love and it's so much harder to watch. Writing this now I realise not for the first or the last time the immense strength Cat had and still has to see this happen to me, to keep herself, and me, on our feet and functioning. It's a visceral experience, an emotional tsunami slamming into your core, and yet you have to, just have to, grit your teeth, steel yourself and be strong. Perhaps this is the true denial, the avoidance, the investment in someone else to take your focus from the gaping hole rent into the reality of your life at that moment. Perhaps we deny so much more than we think?

I know, even as I'm being asked how to get hold of my brother, that no part of me is letting him hear this news like this. The terrible truth is already loose in the world, the media already have a version, they'll add names soon. This is a telling that has to come with a hard hug, a solid embrace, with someone to hold onto as the maelstrom builds. This is news that has knocked me to the ground, but it's my job to protect my little brother, however much bigger than me he now is, from something this hateful and horrid. We leave, but I've no memory of how we managed to drive to the Northeast. I've no idea how I break this news to a mother's youngest son, how this can ever be said with love, what words will ever be enough? No answer at his home, so we head over to the hotel where he works. We have to ask the receptionist to fetch him, we have to pretend we're just passing by and make small talk about how fine the hotel looks until eventually the other staff leave us alone. Then I have to tell him his mother has been murdered.

I love my brother immensely—he's physically one of the strongest people I know, now and then, but this is like hitting him when he's not expecting it, it's a punch to the heart. He visibly staggers, I stumble.

He's incredulous, disbelieving, in shock.

At his desk he logs onto local news sites; "Lytham woman found dead.", It's too early for the terrible words to have formed yet, but it's enough, I can see the light go out in his eyes.

He has calls to make, his partner E. to find. We collect her and head back West.

Our sister rings from the other side of the world. She's already finding snippets on online news sites, has questions none of us can answer. We're not close—but nobody can imagine this being the conversation that would bring three siblings together from around the globe.

Anger. One of my earliest school reports contained the summary "Kelvyn is very quick witted, but he's even quicker to his fists". When you're raised in the constant shadow of violence, when fear and intimidation are your daily diet then anger is never far away. I'd thought the long walk of life had mostly lost that version of me along the way. But, maybe not.

I can still hear the glass smashing. I can feel the receiver crack, fracture and break in my hand as I punch the phone into the wall. I can see Cat, somehow staying strong and together, blocking the door to my office in the showroom and telling a crowd of concerned staff to leave, that I just need a minute, that there's nothing to see. I don't know what I pick up first, but I know I throw everything within reach. That's not great when your office is literally made of glass.

And then it's gone, for now. Cat's hand on my arm, whispered words of love and care. Lost words of magic. Knowing that this must be saved for later. Not knowing how or even if I can force this box to close. Knowing a reckoning will have to wait—but for now I need to be stronger, better, not *that* me. Just for now. The hot flame of anger has saved me so many times, it will again, but now I need to be something else, something more.

It's harder than I can ever put into words. People talk about inner strength, hell I'm sure I have too in these contradictory hops through time, but putting that anger down, the act of crushing yourself inwards like you're making a fist of your soul, biting down, forcing it to recede, clenching your heart, willing your eyes to clear… until you know you're centred, till you can acknowledge the rage, the burning red furnace at the centre of everything, and then, when you must, then look away, look back into the world. I can only say, a decade and more later, it has to have been love that did that. Like the genesis of a cheap comic book superhero, I don't know where the strength to pause came from, to make the flames die down, to step out of the gathering storm. I do know it wasn't mine.

Bargaining. "If only I could. I'd make a deal with God; I'd get him to swap our places".

I've tried to make so many bargains. Again the fiction has lied to us: the police won't look the other way, you can't bribe your way into a prison, it's much harder than you think to buy a gun, the devil doesn't want your soul—even if you'd give it gladly.

I'd give anything to have had my mum call me that night, for me to have been the one to walk through that door first. To have the chance to tell her to just leave. To just have the chance to tell her anything. There's a world of words I want to be able to say but they're all ashes now.

The simple reality is that there's no bargain you can make with anyone other than yourself.

Depression. I think Ms Kubler-Ross was simply too tactful to call this 'reality'. The realisation that you are forever going to be less than you were, less than you could be. That a single moment in time will forever have the ability to pierce your heart, will hold you in its dark thrall forever.

You'll carry this with you evermore—but you might just, with grace, learn to look away.

Acceptance. Never. Not now. Not a fucking chance.

I remember the presence of the officers who came to tell us, if not their names or faces. I remember the certainty.

"Stephen Green murdered your mum".

I also remember that a part of me didn't want to believe them. I could rationalise that certainty—the evidence, the history, the sheer inescapable terror of the scene that poor first officer encountered—the truth of Mum's ending writ in her own blood, the weapon on the floor by Green's drunken hand. I know I knew he'd done it, but I also know a part of me wanted him to be let out of custody so I could ask him myself. I wouldn't have used words.

I'm not sure if anyone has ever applied the Kubler-Ross cycle to the reality of a murder trial before—but oddly enough it works just as well for this survivor's experience of the process.

Denial. Believing this can't be real. Courts, robes and wigs are for fictional entertainments, life shouldn't be like this. At first it seems as if you should only be a spectator, but of course you're not, it's as real as life gets. I spent so long waiting for the villain's last reveal, some ridiculous error by the police, some crazy alibi, the twist at the end of the next cliff hanger episode. It never comes.

Anger. So close to the surface every day. The laughing people in the corridor, the stupid procedures, the wall of armoured glass between me and him. Everything seems set just to fuel that inner fire.

Bargaining. You know that he did it, you know the evidence is incontrovertible, you know the entire prosecution team know this is the surest of sure convictions. And still, so much time hoping to meet the devil at a crossroads, to be able to give a verdict yourself, not to be lost to your peers.

Depression. An eye for an eye is just for fairy tales, you never get her back. Nothing is really fixed by this. Now you've nothing left to make you look to the future. Every day will be less from now on. This doesn't really make you feel any better. And then.

Acceptance. Never. Not now. Not a fucking chance.

The trial, as we were told at the time, and as life has subsequently proven to be true, came around remarkably quickly for a murder case—the prosecution were more than a little confident. The police so clearly understood the pathetic nature of Stephen Green; we were still fearful there was something more. They let a female junior officer lead the questioning of Green—I can remember bridling at the thought they weren't taking it seriously enough, wanting the most senior officer they could muster to sledgehammer the case through the Court—but it was a masterstroke. Green's defence, his versions of what happened that terrible night, it's all so distorted it is literally unbelievable, and yet he continues to condescend as the officer encourages him on. You can see reality strike home a little bit more with each answer he gives, everyone present more perplexed except him. Eventually his frail grasp of what is happening combined with his bizarre superiority behaviours[3] mean that even his own defence team has to treat him as a hostile witness.

The Court turned out to be both dramatic, with the import of our reason for being there, and disappointing in the reality of how it operated. I'd have been alarmed if I'd known who the judge was; Anthony Russell QC[4] had an unfortunate reputation for being lenient, not a quality any of us who exist in the aftermath of such

---

[3] This is now known as the Dunning Kruger effect. It describes a phenomenon in which the incompetent labour under an illusion of superiority because they lack the capacity to accurately assess their own abilities. They're stupid enough to actually believe they're the smartest person in the room.

[4] Anthony Russell QC made national news in scandals in 1996 and 2013

a crime want in a judge. We spent a lot of time at first waiting for procedural matters—walking the streets of Preston looking for good coffee, any coffee, simple distraction—but by Tuesday a jury of twelve had been agreed.

Moments shine clear. I can remember coming face to face with my awful stepfather, my mother's second husband, the person who terrorised my childhood and made it a violent misery, much like his marriage to my mother. Astoundingly (and please understand, my lone reader, I really didn't believe it was possible that I could think any worse of him) he's there as a witness for the defence, a new low by any measurable standard. He's all posture and arrogant swagger for about 3 seconds till it becomes clear I'm about to throw him from the second-floor balcony. Not for the first or last time over the course of these five days I'm grateful for the looming large presence of Nigel— our Family Liaison Officer— he deftly steps forward, puts a very solid arm around me and tells my stepfather to find somewhere else to wait.

I'll always cherish the memory of the look on the face of the Asian lady in the jury—bottom row, two seats in from the right —a perfect line of sight across the barrister's benches to where I'm sat with Cat and Nigel in the family row. The coroner is describing in graphic detail the injuries that have led to Mum's death. The savagery, the frenzy, the cold calculating amount of time spent. There are pictures on a display that no one should ever have to see, images that still haunt my nightmares when the days turn dark. My brother has had to leave for a moment, and behind me in the family rows someone, I don't know who, is gently sobbing, sorrow filling the air. I'm trying not to hurt Cat's hand as my own make fists, sinews flex as I try to slowly pull the arm off the court chair. I can feel the metal edge bending, splitting, feel it cutting deep into my hand. I need it to hurt. Nigel covers my arm with his coat and puts a weighty hand on my knee to say enough, enough now—and in the middle of it, as each word eviscerates a little more of our collective souls, blow after blow, slash following slash, in the midst of all the horror as the steel cuts deep and blood pools in my hand, by happenchance I look up and my eyes meet hers. I'd guess she's a little older than me, the right age to be a mother and a wife, but regardless another human being. Someone I'll never know. Our eyes meet across the courtroom and she mouths the words "I'm so sorry".

It's the first time I can remember thinking of the impact of Mum's murder on anyone outside our immediate circle. To be randomly selected for jury duty and to find yourself sat in a stark formal room listening to a coroner slowly take a human body and life apart piece by painful piece. To see the total absence of remorse, to come face to face with the sort of monster most never meet. And yet to still to have the empathy to reach out in the simplest of human ways. Often, when I need to remember that humans can be the most incredible of species as well as the worst, it's this moment I return to.

It's day 4. We've just come back from the morning break. Oh, that time travelling joy. With a crystal clarity of recollection I can tell you that back in that older reality the Kelvyn sat in the courtroom has flashed far past anger, is making a plan to find someone later and have the sort of conversation that doesn't end well. The me writing this in a coffee shop in the Alps doesn't always recognise that Kelvyn anymore and there's a blessing in that.

We've just come back from the morning coffee break. The foreman of the jury has asked to speak with the usher, who in turn is now speaking to the judge. Us, and both barristers are intrigued. After a brief discussion the judge instructs the galleries to be cleared but tells the families they can stay so as to not cause further concern and upset. It transpires that one of the jurors has told the foreman that another juror has been sending text messages and using his phone during the morning session. Everyone is incredulous. Fortunately judges take this kind of dereliction of duty extremely seriously. Judge Russell even references the disrespect paid to us and then sentences the guy to a night in the cells. But now we don't have the '12 good men and true', but to be fair they're also supposed to be upright, honest and trustworthy. One is clearly a dick. The barristers have a whispered conversation, speak with the usher. Mr Denney[5] comes over – they've agreed to continue with 11 jurors – apparently the Defence Counsel don't think it will make any difference to an "inevitable" verdict. Well colour me perplexed – I'm furious, relieved, intrigued and hopeful. The defence counsel thinks the verdict is "inevitable," and who knew you could have just 11 jurors? I'll add that to the growing list of things I now know that I should never have had to know.

Do you know the difference between right and wrong? Does loyalty affect it? Is it really a subjective measure, or do right and wrong change?

I'm not a saint. I've broken more than my share of minor laws. Ah, so it is subjective? Well, I said minor laws. I can accept that your views and mine on the legality of certain substances might differ. I've certainly put my foot down on roads I thought were empty. Tax—I think I should pay it for all the hours the taxman does—but if I'm working late at night I'm not so sure. Subjective wins to a point.

But right and wrong? I know I wasn't always raised right; a lot of the behaviour I experienced was simply wrong. And inherently I knew. Maybe, just maybe that was due to the shining stars I encountered, the old wise counsel I occasionally got—but I think ultimately, it's because wrong is simply wrong and we know that

---

[5] Stuart Denney QC is the prosecutor. I wish I could tell you more about him, but he's another thing lost.

in the centre of ourselves. And then we make choices, the choices that shape the what of who we really are.

I'm sat in the front row of the family section of the court. Cat sits to my right, my brother beyond her. It's not lost on me that Nigel the family liaison officer is sat on my immediate left, between me and the aisle down which the accused is walked to the dock. Solid, immovable Nigel. On the row behind me are my aunt, uncle, sister and my sister's priest. Behind them are sat members of Green's family. People who've made a choice. Through the course of five days their number gets less. First to leave is his niece, no inheritance is worth this apparently. I can't remember when the others leave, but eventually there are just two left, maybe the rich uncle and aunt whose money Green has always coveted so much, maybe his parents, I don't want to know. I'm steadfastly focused on them not existing. I'm still lost to anger, I'm still too close to that version of me, an eye for an eye seems possibly fair.

Do we stand by someone whatever they've done? Are some things so bad they can't ever be forgiven?

It's the last day of the trial. Our QC is remarkably confident, Green's defence have no idea what to say. For five solid days he's changed his story each morning. He started the week by telling the court that Mum, all 5'3" of her, attacked him, and because he'd watched a lot of king-fu movies (and yes, you'll need to pause in your incredulity) he was able to take the knife from her. At which point she must have fallen on the knife. Again and again and again. By the next morning Mum has apparently run onto the knife whilst he's cooking. It makes less sense, but then, he's had less time to think about it. But by day three we're at the dark heart of it. She deserved it. It was all her fault. She fucking *made* him do it.

Each day we learn more. Much is horrendous, some is banal, and a lot is just pathetically sad. We hear all about his abusive behaviour at bridge[6] club, how Green is a world championship standard player[7], how he belittles mum for not being good enough, for embarrassing him. How he swears and threatens her in public. How many standup members of the community just looked the other way. And bit by bit a picture builds, one none of us saw till it was too late. The testimony and evidence of police, the coroner and so few friends carves a picture of a descent that suddenly seems so inevitable. Horror builds upon horror. We hear how Green has assaulted Mum before. We hear how he's on bail when he actually kills her. How he's seen to repeatedly hit her in the head, just months after she's had brain surgery.

And sat there I hear another list. I listen to a cruel inner voice list how many different times and in how many different ways I let Mum down. So many chances to have put us all on a different path to a different future, forever lost—because I did nothing.

Not once do I leave my seat. Not now, not then, no matter how many times I try to rewrite it in my mind. Why I don't just take out the geriatric prison officer, cross the five metres that separate me from the dock and give Green what he deserves, a decade later I sit and type these words knowing why, still wishing I could have. Fingernails dig into my palm echoing a decade ago. Some things should hurt.

Love. Love saved me then as it saves me now. It will take a decade to know that. A decade to be able to put the anger down and look away. For a moment, then and now, I'm lost to time again—both versions of me at the same time. Love sat next to me, love from long ago and almost forgotten, love taken, love given.

[6] The media will, for reasons too trivial to fathom, latch onto this detail with zealous appeal. Little England.

[7] He's not. He once paid to go on a bridge cruise.

But back then I didn't know that. Love and me were both lost in the dark.

And then it's day 5. Final statements and summing up is done. Now the remaining 11 jurors are sent for lunch and into their deliberations. We rise to leave the courtroom, no idea how long this will take, the usher says we'll be called if and when the jury reach a verdict. Stood in the hall I don't know what we're thinking or doing until I turn and am face to face with the last two people sat in the defendant chairs, the only people left from his family. I pause, start to turn away, it's not their fault however poor their moral compass—and then the man spits on the floor next to me, curses under his breath. Right and wrong. Choices. Love. I walk away.

The papers will later record that the jury take an hour and fifteen minutes to unanimously find Green guilty of murder. They neglect to mention an hour is the lunch recess and it takes five minutes to both leave and enter the court.

30 years. No chance of parole for 23 years.

Judge Russell speaks, he reads from our victim statements. He speaks, for the first time in this dreadful place, of love, of respect. He also speaks about evil and horror, and acknowledges they'll stay with us forever. I would never have expected to be anything other than numb, elated, despondent—but I'm actually held still by his words. It's the first time the word "mum" is used instead of "the victim", the first time in the whole process that she has been spoken of with dignity, that the impact of her loss is acknowledged, rather than just the manner by which it happened. As he speaks Mum is a person again, not just a victim, more than the deceased. I didn't believe that possible anymore. It's fitting, its more than fitting, it's right.

All that is left is to walk out into the fresh air, flanked by counsel and police and to tell the waiting press that it's over. Now we can begin to heal as individuals, as a family. Now it's done.

Except it's not.

V

I am the son of a murdered Mum.

I'm the first-born son, I'm the supposedly capable one, I'm the one with the money, the big successful business, the lawyers on call. I'm the strong one, the one who won't fall apart. It matters least if I do.

I'm the one who let it happen. I'm the one who didn't do enough.

But there is something I can do now. I can make the space to try and let the others heal. There's one last thing I can do for Mum: I can take on the final reckoning of her life. I can sort out her estate, make her final wishes be respected. I walk into it knowingly, gladly. I think it's going to be easy after all we've been through.

And then it takes four more harrowing years.

Mum died without a valid will. Life had changed many times for her, I know it was just a thing she'd let slip, but her circumstances when she was stolen from us meant there was no legally binding record of her wishes. In the horror of emptying her flat, of packing away the broken pieces of her life I took everything, I wanted to know as much as I could. And there, in a box of old papers we found a will we could all agree was right, we knew was what our mum would have wanted. My sister would get all the jewellery. My brother got her car. And I got the most precious gift of all: photographs. Boxes and boxes of photographs.

And that should have been that.

Mum and Green had bought property together, mostly with Mum's money. I simply wanted to split this 50:50, to separate the legal entities of mum's estate and Green quickly and forever. It seemed the only logical approach. I was advised it was the correct legal action. It should have been simple. Except of course Green contested the estate. Murderers can't profit from their crime. My lawyers, old friends who'd already gone above and beyond supporting us, were incredulous. It'll be a nuisance; it'll be dismissed, and you'll move on they said. That's what everyone said.

But.

Green, despite being told he'd no chance of an appeal against his conviction, facing the reality he should die in jail, had more unpleasant ideas. He didn't just refuse to do anything to split the property assets, to let the estate be resolved—instead, he belligerently contested every little decision. There was no law to help or resolve the estate, no law to protect a grieving son from the spiteful and vindictive actions of his mum's murderer. After a year of constant hateful dialogue[8], I sat with my lawyers, sighed a deep sigh, wrote a large cheque and signed the papers to begin litigation against Green in the Chancery court. I'd still no idea what was to come.

Do you remember Ms Kubler-Ross? Well her process assumes you'll move on naturally, albeit all of us at a different pace. But as I was about to find out—sometimes the abyss has other ideas. Sometimes it takes hold.

---

[8] By the end of 2011 Green was calling my lawyers, who were obligated to speak to the man who'd murdered their friend's mum, on a near weekly basis. Neither the prison nor the system seemed able to stop this. And of course, poor Paul was also obligated to tell me every time.

I made the conscious decision to tell my siblings and family as little as I could about what I was going through. I know, God knows I know—it was stupid idea. But. My brother was planning his marriage, my sister had a new family, others were moving on. It was one of the few good things to see. Ostensibly, so were we. We sold our business, downsized from the big house with the big mortgage to a little cottage with none. But emotionally, psychologically I was falling faster and further.

And what seemed so simple wasn't just difficult, it began to look impossible. There really was no law to govern this situation. Almost farcically, Green was a defendant again—and as such didn't have to instruct counsel. He could, and did, defend himself. Which of course gave him access to the prison library, gave him additional phone calls, the hope of days out of his cell. Then, when it seemed it couldn't get any worse, he started writing letters. Addressed to me, sent to my lawyer. Hateful letters that were nothing to do with the estate, everything to do with evil. Eventually I reached out to our old police liaison officer who had a strong word with the prison and they stopped, but not before I found out he'd even written to my grandad. 89yrs old and sent a letter full of bile by your daughters' murderer. It is not often you're glad someone you love has passed away, but I'm thankful he never got to read that letter. I read too many of them.

But that wasn't close to the end of it.

Months slipped by, months that reinforced my role as the son of a murdered mum. As the administrator of the estate I was now the sole focus of Green's attention, his correspondence to my lawyers increased and darkened, none of it sane, all of it deeply unpleasant. Court dates were set, court dates were cancelled. Slowly the case progressed up the ranks of the Chancery court system. Each time we actually got to a hearing the Judge would tell us that the case was wrong, that we were right. They'd agree with every point the estate made… and then they'd defer making a final judgement and move it up to a higher level. Months painfully became years.

Eventually in 2014, four years after he was convicted of Mum's murder, a date was set with a Law Lord to sit in the High Chancery Court of Lancaster Castle. I attended with my barrister and my wife for support. Just post a knee operation I was on crutches and pain medication but, dressed in the same suit I buried my mother in, I gritted my teeth as we were guided through ancient stone corridors to a room heavy with ceremonial importance. Mere feet away from us, flanked by guards sat Green, released again for the day to continue his perverse game.

Proceedings began, our barrister and Green made opening comments. The Lord asked me to take the stand, and I found myself in the dock. I gripped the rail, ready.

And then he let Green question me. You read that right: I stood in a dock and looked the man who murdered my mother in the eye. I knew it was coming, I'd steeled myself, I knew the facts and figures. I thought I was as ready as I could be. Then his first question was "did you know your mum didn't want any of you to get anything from her?" In the incredulous time it took to not answer he followed up with "did you know she hated you all?" It was like he'd been given a knife again. When he started to ask why I wanted to take their marital home off him, the place they'd been happy together, the place he'd need to live when he was released I'd had more than enough. Anger that had simmered for four long years came to the fore. A version of me I thought gone, rose full of rage. I rounded on the Law Lord, furious, asked him how the hell he thought this was appropriate, what on earth was he was doing. Aghast, he just stared at me. I've never been more furious, it took everything to keep my hands on the rail of the dock and say my piece. Two decades of authority, four years of torment, a lifetime of anger—I can't repeat any of the words I said, but I know each and every one was thrown like a punch, meant to hurt. My barrister was certain I was for the cells, I was past caring for their rules.

When we reconvened a genuinely shocked and apologetic Law Lord suspended proceedings; here, so near the end of it all, after four years of moving step by incremental step through the laws of our land this final arbiter of justice had consciously chosen not to read any of the history of the case, to approach it with fresh eyes. He was unaware that he was letting the son of a murdered mum be viciously questioned by her killer. He apologised again and then began to read the long list of the Estate's claim. He found in or favour on every single item and awarded the estate full costs[9]. Everything—all that we'd originally requested four years earlier, for it all to be divided 50:50, the estate given administrative rights to sell the properties. Green removed from our lives.

Unbelievably it takes another year to actually make the judgement legally binding as Green repeatedly tries to appeal, refuses to sign documents and is eventually removed from the process altogether by further legal action. On a wet March morning, five years and three months after Mum was murdered, my barrister calls to tell me it's finally over. On my instruction he sells the properties the next day. Green is financially ruined. The protracted nature of the case, the complexity of an archaic court system, the stupidity and vindictive nature of the defendant all mean that my lawyers 'inherit' slightly more than we do but hell, they earned it.

Stephen Green is finally out of our lives.

---

[9] Anyone who finds themselves in this terrible position will now have James Vs Green to take comfort in, and as an aside, full costs in reality means nothing like that. It's a system that doesn't help victims and survivors and I wanted to make sure I said that at least once.

I am, still, the son of a murdered mum.

It's been the reality of who I am for every day since she died. But now, five years after that terrible day, maybe now there's a chance I can begin to find a way to walk out of the dark.

Chapter 3

Time Travelling

In writing this I've got to acknowledge I'm starting in the middle. So much of the before and after fill these pages, but the middle is the dark heart of it all, the point of convergence from which nothing will emerge unscathed. Yet it's a middle that is also an ending and a beginning, a black hole that has stolen the chance of many possible futures, and the crucible everything before leads to. This is the fatally fixed moment in time I may not have the strength to leave, so it seems to be the only place I could ever really start. I know it will be impossible to ever try and find any truth for the events of that awful night without looking at what brought us to there, and how it shaped all that followed after. Yet now, in this version of my present, before and after seem lost lands forever shaded by that single moment which both obscures and illuminates.

I've thought about the process for long enough to accept that some of the early words have to stay, wrong though they may now be, and many of the latterly wise words seem somehow undeserving when written with the comfortable benefit of revision and review. Finding a way to transcribe the faltering progress of both myself and these words to here has been a psychological puzzlement I'm not sure I've really resolved, but it feels fitting that the telling might just be as confused as I've so often been. It's taken a long decade lost to understand this is one of the darkest traits of depression, one of the unseen ways it takes hold, keeps you down: so much of you lost in the before, the maybe and the wistful wishing of 'different'.

I've spent so long looking back, my inner self caught fast while the outer shell of me stumbled along in the world, both unknowingly looking for things hidden in the dark. Often the sense of any potential future has seemed ethereal, a conceptual hope too elusive to ever actually grasp, the wishful dreaming of a life lost. It's fair to say that my relationship with time is at best difficult, my mind flits from thought to thought almost instantly though they're decades and lifetimes apart. I owe you, my lone reader, an explanation written in my present version of now, yet I've got to also acknowledge that it's something that might well have changed by the end of this journey. My thoughts and memories, these words, they all tumble through time seemingly with no pattern, each collision sparking a potential new connection, another possible destination. Whatever their genesis they all inevitably and unforgivingly circle back to the beckoning absence in the middle, the moment that's now the lens to everything else.

It's the first day of a new decade, the second coming of a roaring 20s. I'm sat in the darkening afternoon of northern England staring at a screen trying to coax the very words you're reading now into existence, hoping to find some intellectual sense of forward. Yet at exactly the same moment, at every moment, it's forever that inescapable January day in 2010 and I'm smashing the receiver unconsciously, the internal storm already reaching a crescendo unbidden. I'm again stood there in the shattered ruins of her life, and as the glass smashes I'm again a small boy, decades earlier, flying towards a wall thrown in a rage I can't fathom. I guess I'm too young to understand the concept of time—and time, it would seem, in any ordinary sense, is forever fractured. The more I understand that I need to try to look to a possible future, any future, the more I'm drawn back to the past to try and conjure a reckoning. The harder I look for any clarity in my understanding the more the ripples become waves overlapping, distorting, enhancing, hiding. Did the toddler getting thrown through the air by a cruel stepfather who wanted him gone know he would become the son of a murdered mum? The logically linear answer would seem to be no, but how can that ever be a certainty? Why would we consider that certainty a truth when it's the same fallen son sat in an alpine coffee shop trying to navigate the lay lines of destiny that seem to connect child abuse so obviously to domestic violence, and on to a terrible sense of self?

If one moment right in the heart of it all has darkened the future, if it can cast such a clinically harsh light into the past… then what else might flow with it?

It will help to understand early on that the words which document my journey to now weren't formed in any logical procession through time. I didn't start at the beginning and finish at the end. There's a me in that coffee shop in the Alps writing forlorn words to be read in the future, a me that is intrinsically linked by the gravity of one moment in time to a me wandering lost in the world shaping old words with his ghosts, to the me high on a cliff focusing on every grain of granite to avoid looking at what he's written here today, who is still the me sat in the Westmorland Dales shaping all of these words right in this moment of now. So many of the eventual words are drawn from an as yet undiscovered future, a me that is yet to come. More have slowly come into focus now and some from times far before are still waiting to be written. Each of those versions of me are very different and yet the same, each are now shaped by the memories of the other. It's easiest to understand how the me that exists since the loss of Mum can be so defined by the how and why of it; it's harder to explain how the me from before then has come to be so as well. Some sentences started a decade ago still wait to be finished, others still don't know if they have a future. Words fresh written yesterday lie right at the very beginning of the journey to today.

Right up to that moment I, like most people I'd guess, had thought of time as simply a linear eventuality—the past pushing us through the present into a future, ever moving us along. I could give a cursory nod to actuality and the cheery concept of our choices informing the direction of travel, but—and I can laughingly hear my fool self saying this so many times—I truly believed we were born with forward facing eyes so we didn't have to look at that which lay behind us. I guess I had more reason than most to hope the past was dead, buried and gone with its secrets locked in little boxes, unopened, forgotten. I had no idea that to ever move forward I'd have to go back.

Einstein proposed time as constant, simply existing in all entirety. Absolutely infinite in its version of being. I've had so many long dark nights to read and question and explore, I know that's too simple—but it's also not the truth of my experience. I think time exists only within us, our energy affecting our interaction with it, its viscosity changing based on our own inputs, each of us stars in an unknowable firmament, each affecting the other and in turn affected by so much we can't know. Einstein largely ignored the existing belief in Newtonian Schema, that time had a *flow*. He proposed a time that was both static and in constant flux, all things at all times. But over the last ten years, which I've used as a lens to look at a life, I've come to see if not understand that there are indeed infinite invisible currents that flow through each of our personal versions of time, much like even the wildest of rivers. The seemingly inescapable depths that pull at you, those calm still parts that are so seldom acknowledged, fiercely bright moments that rage past in full spate, maelstroms that hold hard until, beyond or for not quite long enough. We each have the capacity to be more than just a single star, we can be complex galaxies in an infinite universe, multiple versions of ourselves. I'm often adrift in time; there are days I manage to swim, I believe there are days of grace to come, but there have been many days when I drown, time like a vast weight of water slowly crushing the life from me, making it hard to rise, harder to hope, impossible to escape. I appreciate Einstein's simultaneous actuality but I also feel the ebb and flow of Newton's procession. There's a vortex that wants to pull everything in and hold it fast, and there are other currents that tear the most precious moments from you never to be found again. The further I fall, the higher I climb, the more I feel time may well be Larkin's ephemeral echoed axe, aware and unknown, never to be grasped.

And any life could be like this I know. The raging river with the pausing pretence of calm, the days the swift waters abate and everything schematically just flows. Life, love, loss. The day-to-day inertia of simply being, the glory of being more for an all too brief moment, the reality of being a rat in the wheel. I can push on, I can plan, but ever so often, down in the deep currents, the sense that forward is an illusion stirs, that maybe all we ever do is circle the pit hoping not to disappear forever. Yet I have to accept that all of that is within each of us, my tsunami at times not even a ripple in your flow, yet your gentle eddy able to hold me still in my storm. Though we may not see it, we each carry the power to affect the other.

A decade and a lifetime later, having come so far and yet so often still anchored fast by the cruel actuality of events, I've come to believe that time is a gloriously gifted illusion. The linear progression is an escapist blessing we might choose to buy into, for some, too few, a lucky reality; for some, too many, a trick we never quite manage to master. Yet Einstein's totality of time is also a fool's paradise—I've tried with my everything to reach that one moment again, to find a way to alter all that follows. It'll never happen. All I can ever hope is to find a way to change my perception of it.

But. A moment of time-spun revelation, I wrote those words up there *then*, never imagining that I'd come to know what I do *now*. Now I'm far further away in many a sense, words revisited, seen afresh, proven possibly true. So did then make now? Or have I revisited it to prove a point to myself?

All I can ever hope is to find a way to change my perception of it.

Perhaps that's where the old magic lies, the magic that underpins the unknown. If I can indeed change my perception of it, really change it on the psychological level, change my emotional response to it then perhaps, as if indeed by magic, I'll have changed time. It's a hope.

The past holds the bad times fast; loss, regret and worse all reside there. The future speaks of hope and holds the promise of choice. Yet, if I'm to walk forward into light then I need to find the hope in my past and the strength to accept an unknown future.

Words written then to say something to a future me, words that don't even mention now.

Time travelling becomes easier when there's a fixed point you can never escape. No longer a simple sequence of memories, everything is measured by its proximity to that one moment, by the intensity associated with it. I can tell you more about the seconds immediately after I took the call than the days and weeks that followed. I know every detail of the hours in court but can't tell you who was at the funeral. I know that I've spent longer thinking about my mother's final moments than I have about anything else in my entire life—I can tell you I haven't spent even a fraction of the time thinking about it that my mother endured.

That one moment in time seemingly steals from everything else. It twists, distorts, burns into realities unrecognisable, unavoidable and undeniable. To put anything into any sense of chronological order seems the task of a fool, to measure it by anything other than impact offers no real sense of meaning or import. No other measure feels either possible or right. As I hit my fiftieth year it seems such an unworthy measure of time compared to knowing it's a decade since she was killed. My own birthday now means far less to me when it's come to mean so much to celebrate hers.

Consequences ripple forward, but I've come to believe they might well ripple backwards. Is it really the event or its impact on the self at the centre? Is it reality or confirmation bias to link the dark moments through time—did one lead to another? Did the failure to act then lead to the outcome there? Is my mind simply wandering lost in the neural pathways of remembrance – if I can flit from this moment to the next, if I can leap so far back… is there a way to alter the outcome? I know I'll never bring her back, but can I absolve my soul? Does redemption lay hidden somewhere in the understanding? Does understanding happen through knowing or feeling? Now that I need to actually believe, I fear I've lost my capacity for faith.

Fingers fly across a keyboard as moments are pulled free of time's restrictive context. Words from decades ago taking shape, little boxes long locked prised open with the crude crowbar of necessity and need. I need to find a way past this.
I need to find answers that aren't based in the emptiness of risk, lost in my loss I'm just wise enough to know there has to be a

better way yet I'm too scared to pause in the flow, to brace and hold in the moment. I need to say enough. I can hope to revisit moments when I've found a way for them to hurt less. I know that a reckoning has to come – in the process of writing I'll need to review – take a scalpel to the cancers I'm feeding, to make some form of sense – perhaps picking open old wounds is the self-harm I seem to need to focus myself into now, perhaps this is a more cerebral version of pushing myself towards the cliff's very edge.

There have been dark moments—moments when it's been nearly impossible to see a path forward, moments when the reality of never being able to make a deal with a God that has clearly left the building crashes home. Yet in those moments something has drawn me on. Hope? Quite possibly, though I know that seemed gone for the longest of times. So is it plausible that the echo of future happiness has sent ripples back along the pathways of life? Is it possible love transcends time? That hope really knows no bounds? When you're lost in the dark they seem like impossible concepts, yet it also seems like any kind of salvation will only be found somewhere in the unknown.

It's a cold winter day somewhere in that dark decade, my head is down, the wind howls with ferocious glee. I'm making my way upward, just me and my ghosts, heading towards a favourite place, striving for a moment of empty, the chance of forcing a peace, quieting the voices if only for a while, simply lost to the concentration of risky endeavour. Right now I'm in the relative calm of the cirque, soon a decision will be called from me by simple geography. Except there's no decision to make. Just a few hundred metres above me the storm is waiting to welcome me and I know there's an edge sharp with consequence looming large out of sight. I feel in my bones that's where I need to be today. I've only seen people turning back, yet today that won't be me. This is one of the dark days when I need to feel risk's razor cut deep. As I reach the shelter of this high place the tarn is lost from sight as flung flurries sting their way across the water. The steepening flanks rise sharply, they offer enough shelter for a cold solitary couple to be huddled making plans to wisely retreat. As they depart looking questioningly in my direction, I sort my kit, I change my gloves, put on goggles and get out the axes. I need to push on, upwards towards the storm. I have to try and overload my senses, break down my own defences for the chance to find the place of emptiness inside. I need to feel something other than this, to be momentarily alive again, to banish everything else if only for a while. I need to move on. So much of me is forever then. I need to be somehow more here, more now.

A surprising sound calls me from my reveries, takes my attention away from jangling nerves objecting to doing this again. Out of the swirling towards me comes an implausible joyous sight—a family out in the hills on this vile day, bowed against the wind yet somehow all smiling and laughing together in their festive bobble hats. It's impossible not to brighten at the infectious sound of them happy together. Another me makes an appearance and I tell their young son that he has the best hat of the day, he grins and high fives me, I point out the way down and they wish me well with no idea of my plan. Even in my own dark I'm brightened by their light for a moment. Then I press on up into the storm hoping to find an internal silence for a while.

There's enough verglas to feel like a roll of the dice, crampons have just enough bite to make me feel luck could be on my side. At the infamous gap I hop across confident this is where I belong, moving well. As the rock rises and the snow banks out to steep I find myself paused exactly in the moment. Axe embedded above me; weight nicely balanced on front points. Not quite cragfast, not really flowing. Consequences call from the swirling depths beneath my feet. Windblown fragments of ice sting with a welcome sensation of danger. The moment stretches out. I'm then and now, before and after. All of me is in this very moment. There's a tired old me that knows I've climbed this route many many times. There's a far younger sounding me that doesn't believe it can go wrong on a route this low in the grades. An occasionally wise me knows I've never been here in exactly this moment before, may never again. Younger me goads older me, wiser me is new to the party but has his say. The knowledge of the past strengthens today with the hope of a better tomorrow, I hear the laugh of those future happy children, today it's louder than the lament of lost love and the voices of recrimination. Pause, settle into the very real reality of now, focus on that happy sound. Breathe in, breathe out. Let the calm grow. Ignore the cold, feel the mountain with all of you, feel each steel point of connection, forget the doubts, let all the weight drop away, simply be this. Be right here, be right now. Move when you're ready, move with grace, feel a solid part of now, climb well, climb until consequences fade away like memories torn free by the wind. All of me is right here in this moment, if only for a moment, once more. And then climbing turns to walking, the edge fades to flat and the blind white flanks of the fell beckon me on to an indistinct summit and the turn for home. Me, myself and I are finding our way bit by bit, navigating our way through time together. Yesterday and tomorrow are somehow helping me survive today.

Are these the tiny incremental steps that have begun to shape my journey? Have they fed just enough good into the dark days for my inner me to still be there somewhere? Are these the moments that drew me on into the unknown? If the dark can shade before and after then I have to hope the light can find a way to brighten both too. I have to remember what it is to fly on those wings of hope, to believe in better. I have to find a way to balance loss, love, failure and regret. To somehow balance then with now.

Displaced a decade forward I know there's indeed a now waiting that is so much brighter than any I could envisage then; looking back I can all too easily recall how dark those days were, that they're still there, waiting to welcome me back into their embrace. And yet. I made it from there to here, then to now. I also know I'm only now strong enough to really look into the abyss and know that I can turn away, that I can risk opening long buried boxes in the knowledge I can also close them. I often still think I don't know where that strength came from; I know I'll discover I do, by searching through time.

Sat looking back with hindsight's supposed wisdom it's all too easy to connect the dark moments together to build a picture with an inevitable ending, but the truth is that no-one trapped in those moments saw it coming. The final reveal stole up on us and nothing would ever be the same.

For the longest time I thought I was lost, and for the longest time I was sure I didn't deserve to be found. Like any failure walking to the gallows, I thought my fate was one I'd brought upon myself. It took an understanding only developed by slipping through time to see that I was still surrounded by love, that there were signs and stars from before, after and then—all helping to show me the path ahead, the wandering way I'd come to find myself again.

I know there will be people stronger than me who've made this journey alone. I also know that I couldn't have made it without the people who helped me keep my own flame alive. What I've struggled to fathom for so long is that I'd not yet met many of them when they lent me their strength, that some of them were long since lost to me and a precious few were already ghosts.

It's October 2009. I'm sat in the upstairs window seat, lunch is in the Aga, I've not opened the wine yet. The phone rings. It's a Sunday and my mother is calling. I could ignore it, I could call back to suit me, but I answer, we don't speak enough.

It's a tough call to take. My mother tells me her husband has hit her, hit her enough that the police are involved. I'm incredulous: any rage doesn't come till later, so unexpected is this to hear. Has he no idea what I'll do to him? This couldn't be more unbelievable if the little creep had taken a swing at me.

But.

My mother is full of apology. "It's not the real him", "it's been blown up out of proportion" and everyone's halcyon favourite: "it'll never happen again"

"Leave the apartment now."

"Come stay with us."

"I'll keep you safe."

The melancholic wishing of regret-laden memories makes we want to believe all or even any of those words were said. Now's knowledge of what will follow, what has already happened in the past of that now, means I have to accept they weren't. Or at best, they weren't said well enough.

I could have pushed more, I should have made that happen, I didn't. And though I don't know it then, though I still struggle to escape it now, that was when I opened the door to everything that would happen later, that was when I became complicit in all that followed, that's another moment that will come to damn me. Another moment in time burning too fiercely to dim and fade, it obliterates all the other moments around it until it's all I know of then, and so much of what shades today.

There's a pattern to domestic violence. It's one of repetition and escalation, it's one of isolation and exclusion.

Months later he follows my mother into a police station, lifts her off her feet and pins her to a wall with his hands around her throat. And no-one tells us. Not a word.

Mum says nothing.

Her friends say nothing.

The police say nothing.

At the point when he kills her he's on bail—but there's no support process put in place, no quiet word, no aftercare, nobody takes a single extra step to make sure it doesn't happen again. We're a society that all too often chooses to claim a blind eye. What happens behind closed doors doesn't get talked about. No one does anything to make her safe.

It's not their job.

No: it was mine. It was society's. And we failed. I failed.

I've been the son that would have knocked you to the ground for a funny look.

I've been the son who'd sit and hold a stranger's hand as they slipped off this mortal coil.

And when it mattered most I was neither. I've looked through all of my time to try and understand the what and the why of where I was when I was really needed and there's nothing.

When it really mattered most, I wasn't there.

On the dark days I can't escape *then*. That's just how it is. There are many days when here isn't my now, when my reality doesn't place me in the physical world, rather my inner self wanders lost in the ruined remembrance of yesterday. On the days when the weight of before is simply overwhelming I can't move on. It holds me fast and time just flows over and around me, the axe echoes distant, unknown. It takes everything to simply stay, not to give in and fall—physically, psychologically, emotionally. The dark days tell me in no uncertain terms this is where I belong. When someone depressed tells you they just don't have the energy to get up it isn't because they're weak— it's because you can't begin to imagine the weight of what they're trying to carry. It is literally crushing the life out of them.

Those are the days when you need to find a candle in the dark. Those are the days when you have to hope the distant stars will shine for you, that you've just enough left to notice, enough left to believe there's a way out of the past. You might not have the strength to make or even begin that longest walk. In the worst of it, hope is the tiny flame you need to keep alive.

For so long I fuelled that flame with hate and anger. Just as it began to flicker out in me I realised love was what would really keep it alive.

Chapter 4

Voices in the dark

I

How do you fight the monsters within when you begin to believe that one of them may well be the real you? Who do you talk to when you have things to say that no one should ever hear? Why would you ever choose to speak words of hate to the ones you love?

That there are horrors in the world is one of the hard lessons we all learn as we grow up. That those horrors might impinge upon our lives is a reality many of us will sadly face. But when I began to listen to the voices in the abyss, voices that spoke of guilt and assigned blame, voices that longed for violent vengeance, voices that wove their own worst versions of an already distorted truth—that was when I came closest to being lost for good.

There are images burned into me that I can't ever unsee. There are imagined horrors made worse in the not knowing, and there are unimaginable horrors in the knowing that I'd give anything to forget. I'd deserve to hate myself evermore if I tried to forget any part of it for even a moment.

I have terrible thoughts of terrible deeds. I wrap myself in them for comfort. I welcome them when I'm alone. I have nightmares filled with screams and blood. I have hopes and dreams filled with screams and blood.

A decade later these sentences have sat here, some of the first I ever wrote, some of the only words to stay from the lost times immediately after Mum was murdered. I've slowly deleted the worst of them as I've fought my way free of the me that wrote them, yet these last ghosted thoughts of a worse me remain, the self-harm scars I inflicted on my inner self. I've known they are words which must be acknowledged, that in finding a way to unsay them I might find a way to be free of them, free of what they say of me. They've been some of the last words revisited, even if their genesis burns right there in those awful early days of falling. They're the cruel desire of the fire I thought would cauterise the hole in my heart. They're words that drove me on, drove me to break myself, to lose myself. They're words I've run both from and towards.

I know now that these are words that speak the language of the way I was raised, the formative lessons of a bad childhood. They are words that tell so much of how we lost Mum, words of violence. They say all of how I came so close to losing myself; wanting to be a terrible me so nearly, eerily like the other men in my mother's life. The path to redemption lies in relinquishing these words, refusing to let them define who I am or who I might become. I have to be better than those awful men, to become a better son, a better me.

I've lain there in the dark thinking the most terrible thoughts —and these haven't been the things that kept me from sleep, they're not the things I've woken nightmared from, they've been my solace. A longed-for hope of retribution, they've seemed a fair price for a soul valued so little I'd gladly have traded it away for a moment alone in the dark with him. I came so close to embracing them. Not that I could ever have made them real—but they could have stolen away the last of me. A double win for hate.

What does it do to your soul to want to kill another person? To truly, with all of you, want to exact a revenge that blow by blow, slash by slash matches the evil of the act already done. Movies, literature, and the opinions of strangers echo the mantra of an eye for an eye, yet what toll does this take on the self? I can tell you how many years, months, weeks and days it is till he's released. Imagining plans for vengeance, I lay beside my love, oblivious to the cost of true loss, too stupid to value what I still have more than that which I've lost. Over the years, I've erased countless thoughts, discarded harsh hopes and wicked wishes—all the while falling short of the person my mum and those I love deserve.

Even now, so far out into the light, sat rewriting this on the flanks of Riggindale's rounded ridge, closer to my best me than in a decade, I can feel the pull of the dark, the easy wishing of vindication, the resentful depression of inaction. As the wisest philosopher of my age once said, "anger leads to hate and hate leads to the dark side". But it starts with fear. Fear that you'll never be able to live with yourself.

For so long, I've stumbled through these thoughts, revisiting them too often or perhaps not enough. I've spent so long avoiding being defined by the words of others, in seeking to define myself, without acknowledging those words that define so much of my past, the way I was raised. I should know there are better words, better ways to be, better futures to plan. This version of me does. This version of me doesn't. It changes depending how each night goes.

In my darkest moments, I clung to these words, seeking solace in the distraction of the impossible. I've punched walls until my knuckles bled, balanced myself right on the razor edge of consequence, yearning for a different pain, anything to avoid confronting the very heart of it.

Regret laid bare.

For so long violence was the answer. It was a life lesson learned the hard way when I was young. Fight or fall. Meet anger with more anger. Get up one more time. Hit first. Hit last. Make sure your bite is much worse than your bark. Violence was never the answer, I just never learned the right questions.

That's a lie.

I learned them long ago.

They're just so difficult to ask.

Violence is easy, quick, a fleeting solution for a wounded heart.

It's the long dark hours of the night. It's 2010. It's 2015. It's 2019. It's any and all of the bad times held fast by the abyss, unable to see past the hate. It's walking in the light of a beautiful day in a beautiful place with the beautiful people you love, knowing you carry an ugly darkness deep inside you hidden.

But for now let's say it's the long dark hours of any night. Time is weaving other realities into existence again. It's the long dark hours of the night and again my mind is racing, avoiding, distracting. The darkness holding me down hard, ever to the same place. Thoughts, and none of them good, fight to be the loudest inside my head—tongue bitten hard to keep them locked inside. Why didn't you? How couldn't you? You should have, you could have. You let it happen. It's your fault. You don't deserve this life you're living now, how dare you think you could be happy again?

But this far forward in time I now know the truth lies deeper, I need to look further down.

The worst monster in the dark isn't that embodying what I didn't do. It isn't the old false answer of violence or its easy animal attraction. It's the what I didn't do of something else.

The reality is mum never told me about the abuse because she knew the truth of that me: "Kelvyn is quick to his fists". Repulsive as it is to contemplate it, her own truth was that she loved Green and was afraid of what I might do to him—what that would do to her. Violence wasn't the answer. Violence was the problem. It's always been the problem.

Circling. Avoiding. Distracting.

Half a truth.

Deep at the bottom of my abyss I can hear a callow taunting laugh, the sound of a self, loathed—beckoning me further down still. Why couldn't she tell you? Why didn't you know? What sort of a person can talk to a stranger through the last moments of their life and not have the conversation that would have kept their own mum alive? What does it say about you that she couldn't tell you?

That so much of this came as a shock, as we sat in the court and heard the horrors unfold. The empty chair. The inevitability to it all. Violence begetting violence. Would she be here still? Would the pattern have repeated again and again? All it would have taken was a conversation. An honest and connected conversation. The sort of conversation you've been trained to do, spent decades doing with strangers.

The sort of conversation a son and his mum should be able to have.

But.

When it mattered most you weren't even listening.

II

For nearly all of the 1990's I spent my Saturday nights either clubbing with Generation X, sleeping at the crag or manning the telephone lines at the Manchester Samaritans on Oxford Road. I was young and male, and I got the 'prized' Saturday night shift in the city that parties hard. I remember telling a sweet old lady at the induction day that I'd not had the best of starts in life, that I'd lost friends, understood abuse, I would be unphased and understanding, consciously empathetic. And I really believed that. Brace. Brace. Brace. It took till just 3am on my very first unsupported overnight shift, nerves raw from a call too awful to comprehend. I switched off my line and went for a walk and, for the first time in a long time, took the sad cigarette I was offered by the other wise old volunteers on call that night. I lit it, looked at it burning in my hand, menace bright in the dark and recalled what I'd just been told about another dreadful stepfather and his appetites and his cigarettes. I threw it away just before I threw up. Over the rest of a decade it got easier, I got better at letting it go, and in doing so I was able to offer more. It's not about persuading, belief or advice. It's about simply being there, about really listening, letting the person on the other end of the line be really heard, letting them know that you care, that the world cares. And maybe, on occasion, being the kind companion at the end. No judgement. Just unconditional positive regard, love if you will. I knew all of that two decades before we lost mum.

But when it mattered most I wasn't even listening.

That's the truth at the bottom of the abyss. That's what lies waiting in the dark. That's why I deserve to be lost.

How do you look away from that?

There's a lot of nonsense spoken about mental health. You need to be diagnosed. You just need to snap out of it. It's disrespectful to say you're depressed when other people are suffering more. You can't be depressed because you look so happy.

It's a spectrum. A very individual and personal spectrum that only the person concerned can ever really know all the details of. Yet they're also the person who might well find it hardest to acknowledge. These words can only ever be my truth, but I've spoken them enough now to know they touch at least part of the experience of everyone who's ever been lost in the dark; when you simply can't look away from the abyss, when it whispers to you all of the time, when you carry it everywhere with you—that's what depression means to me. And as it crushes you it magnifies all the bad—the self-loathing, the guilt, the hate—and it makes it desperately difficult to see the good, any good, anything else at all.

It takes the light from your world.

III

Today I went for walks with the two dogs in my life.
In the low morning sun of a hopeful day I wandered out of the new gate in the back wall with the most beautiful white dog in the world: Pushka, Queen of Ellersyde, our long-lived husky dog. Much like me she now has good and bad days, but on a day like this, even here in her twilight times, it's a special privilege to walk beside her, to see her leap, snuffle and stalk (I choose not to see the slips, stumbles and falls). To listen to her howl the song of her kind into the wind, a sound of pure joy, it's a chance to be truly connected to an elemental wonder. To watch her is to remember what it is to be a wild free spirit full of grace. To watch her now is to really understand what it is to love something you'll have to love enough to say goodbye. Just not today, I'm not that strong yet.
We didn't go far, but we went far enough. Up to the big fallen tree,

slowly, at a pace to suit, but together, each singing in our own way. We're doing our very best to make these last fading days together the very best of days.

Then, with Pushka happily asleep in her bed I packed a rucksack and set off to find a big hill. It's been nine months since the elective ankle operation that so nearly robbed me of the chance to ever wander in the wonder again. It still hurts, it aches, it complains, it tells me I can't. It's made manifest the very worst of my self-doubt, it speaks of possible loss and the loss of the possible. Some days, most days, I've started to believe I've crippled myself; I've thrown away the chance of a life I love. I often wonder if I'll ever be more than broken again. I often think that this is the karma I deserve. That in losing Mum I deserved to lose myself. That I don't deserve to be happy. So many conflicting thoughts, an ever-present noise that fogs my mind. Some days I wonder if… that's it. Just if.

He wasn't invited, he's never invited, but I knew the black dog would come along for the ride. He'd want to be there if I stumbled, he'd want to push me if I slipped, to howl in glee when I fell.

He'd want to tell me he was right all along.

Parked in Grisedale I made my way in breathtaking light up onto the fellside—the long steady climb to the Hole-in-the-Wall my aim. Dollywaggon and Nethermost glowered gloriously with their cloud-shrouded tops in front of me, urging me ever onwards, reminding how I fell in love with the high places and why they mean so much to me, celebrating why I'm not ready to let them go, giving me a reason to pick the right fight. In every direction ridges and edges soar steeply upwards, speaking of the possibility of future adventures, reminding me why I need to rage andkeep the light alive.

The black dog, as I suspected, stayed hidden just out of sight, a low growl nearly heard on the wind, just enough hint of a bite to let me know he was there.

He's a cowardly dog, nearly never appears when other people are there. Prefers the long, lonely hours of the night to the bright light of day, doesn't really want to share me, wants to have all of my attention. Feral, he wants to separate you from your pack, wants to pick on you when you're at your weakest, stalks you in your blind spot. He's the dog that slinks up unseen, nips you, nudges you, bites you. The song of his kind isn't one of joy— it's the long drawn-out howl of what might be, the short sharp snap of what's lost. He's not an honest dog either; his version of events always speaks the language of the abyss, always sounds far worse than it should, promises a bite that'll hurt more than you can possibly bear. But he is persistent. My, is he persistent. And if you listen to his song long enough, it takes a siren's hold, calls you in to the dark, holds you down in the depths. The black dog wants you to question yourself, second guess your choices, to give up without one more try; even better, don't try in the first place, don't think you can.

But the journey of the last few years has taught me this: he's a lazy dog. He's not made for the long walks, he doesn't like the high places. This may well hurt me physically, but there's a good chance it'll hurt him more. As I make my way across Grisedale Brow, even now pushing myself to go faster and harder, the black dog falters and shrinks, is somehow less. The ankle feels good for now, and I know that saps the dog's strength still further. When pain stabs at me I can feel him growl with glee, urge me to stop, tell me to quit. But I now know to pause, centre, regroup. Focus out not in, be in this moment, not those, practice the hard-found mindfulness of now. I connect with what really matters, I give thanks. I have to master this pain, I have to make it mine, maybe not ever a good thing, but maybe my thing. The winning of this will be in knowing the pain is only a part of the whole, not the all of me. If I know that, really know, then maybe it and the damned black dog won't have dominion over me. Maybe I'll be free.

As my exertion makes the black dog falter I'm finally able to look up, to start to make my own choices about the route ahead. I'm well past my originally intended goal, I head higher in hope. Metaphor hangs heavy as I pick the most obtuse line, take the steps closest to the edge. Confidence growing, I'm able to look down into the void and smile in remembrance of what might yet be again. With my hands firmly on the solid rock I know I've got this, today isn't a day when the easy enticing pull of quitting will win, today I'm free of the weight of doubt.

Here in the high places, with consequence looming large, I'm again the one in control and the dog looks scared. I laugh for the first time in far too long. Other ghosts tell me of love, let me know I can carry on, tell me I will get there. I'm back where I belong, I'm at peace, I'm my best me again even if only for a while. I like that, it's been too long, far too long. I'm striding out and past the edge now, the summit beckons me onward, into the future. This isn't a place where the black dog holds any power, today this is my place. Today that's enough.

There's a thing about being depressed that surprises the folks lucky enough to not have met their own black dog out on the trail; for so many people it doesn't show. I'd already stopped wearing black, I've always listened to The Smiths and I was and am (I like to think) really good company. My inner Eeyore is a very private soul, keeps to himself. My darkness isn't contagious, rather it deepens, reinforces itself, spreads its infection to all the corners of my psyche. Often the wider I smiled, the more I laughed, the harder I pushed ...the worse I actually felt inside.

And of course there's another dichotomy therein; when you look the picture of health and happiness the passing world, even those closer to you, they all think you're fine. And of course you tell them that you are. When you love those you spend your time with the very last thing you want is to pull them down into the dark with you. A problem shared feels like a problem you weren't strong enough to deal with on your own – another failure, another of the little losses that slowly steal away your sense of worth. To be in those simplistic linear terms so far from that black hole and to still feel so firmly held fast, to have come so far physically and to have not moved on, it's crushing.

Slowly as the mountains began to help me recover a sense of self that I thought I might just be able to rebuild a life around them, it almost imperceptibly got more difficult to acknowledge to others the weight I was carrying. When you build yourself into an image of strength and capability it's just one more defeat to admit to others, or even yourself, that you're struggling.

But.

The mountains had other ideas. Mountains are places that ultimately demand a truth from you.

As I pushed myself to achieve more in those mountains, as old injuries returned to be counted, I began to understand I had to lighten the load, I had to be able to focus on the what and why of my oft dangerous where: I had to be really present in the moments. And I had to do it not just for me, but for those I climbed with, for those I left at home, for those no longer here, those I still hear. As the mountains helped me glimpse the me I could and should be they made me begin to realise the true value of now.

I had just enough sense to know what I didn't know. I had just enough good fortune to find wise counsel, to have friends who held the rope metaphorically and physically. And I continued to push, I thought I had to burn so bright – peak followed peak. Unacknowledged the abyss got deeper.

IV

"This too shall pass". It's somewhere in 2016. I'm sat with this lovely guy discussing a project and I know I've drifted, I'm only ambiently participating, my focus now elsewhere, lost in those words that are tattooed on his arm. I know all too well the secret code they speak of, the fight he's had or (more likely) is still going through. And I can so utterly understand it, applaud it, wish him well. And in the dark inside me a voice wants to laugh out loud;

"No, it fucking won't mate"

I'm so practiced at keeping it in now, smiling on the outside.

"You'll carry it on your back forever until it breaks you".

Smile. The conversation flows, deadlines, ideas, progressions and plans. I like the guy, I really do. Focus on that. Today's a good day for him, he's making his own light. I don't know him well enough to know what lies waiting in his personal darkness, what it is that looks back at him from his own abyss. I like the guy, focus on that. He's happy, full of enthusiasm for the project, ideas tumbling forth. He's happy, focus on that. Bring yourself back to here, smile, laugh, try to mean it. Engage in the moment.

Its January 15th, 2020. A decade gone. So much different, so much I thought I could never change. I grit my teeth as a caringly careful young lady etches a scar I'm proud of onto my arm forever. Words I've slowly brought to life in my heart, words I've come to see as a vital part of my own truth, words that have kept a hopeful flame alive in the dark. *Scars only heal in the light.*

Words can be a weapon. So often they were a precursor to violence in my youth. With my stepfather, you'd come to recognise the pattern, know the triggers, seemingly good words said with bad intent. Words that were the forewarning of where events were heading, words that were his foreplay to violence. Words sneered, malice meant, solicitous questions with no right answers that might help you escape what was coming. Words intended to hurt just as much as the punches and the kicks. Psychological abuse to bruise all the way down to your sense of self. This was the violence that opened the door to so much worse for my mum, this was the way he broke any understanding of what love should be, what it really is.

But, ever and always, real truths are only ever found when you see both sides.

Words can be an embrace, they can lift you up just as physically as they knock you down. Words of love are the spell that lets you fly. They're the given strength that push your hands into the ground as you get up one more time, they're the shield that protects the you trying to survive inside. Words of love spoken once but remembered when long faded away can be the most precious thing in the world, a lifeline of hope just as you drown. They can be impossible to hear, they might fall on momentarily-deaf ears but if you can learn to accept them and carry them forward with you then they can be everything.

The abyss got deeper whatever my petty achievements, no matter how far I travelled, how much I pushed. Until I began to talk about it. With loved ones, with friends, and even with strangers. It wasn't and isn't easy, but it is safer than so many of the options I used to think were better.

Talking to someone about this can be the hardest thing you might ever do; it might also be the best. Says the person tapping into a keyboard late in the night… but really it can.

You're so alone, no one will understand, it's not happened to them, they can't really know, they'll think you're… and then they don't.

You're not alone.

People are empathetic.

They will understand.

You'll become stronger.

A trouble shared isn't ever close to a trouble halved, but it is reduced. It becomes a trouble acknowledged, brought into the light, a trouble made less by the saying. Talking about it just once makes it so much easier to talk about it the next time, and each time you do you get stronger and it gets less. I guarantee it's not the end. Life is full of new beginnings. I'm certain change can be a positive. There's always a way.

I promise it can get better. I know because it did.

But... it starts with you. Pick up the phone and call a friend. Pick up the phone and call a stranger. Pick up the phone and ask for help. Talk to someone, anyone.

For me, violence never really fixed anything. For the longest time I thought it was just the violence that made me strong. I was never bigger or faster in a fight. I used to pick fights because I was small and people thought they'd win. But I always got back up and that was usually enough. But resilience without adaptation eventually leads to fatigue. If you go and go and go again with no hope of a destination then eventually you fall however strong you think you are.

Words could have fixed everything.

Words of love would have fixed everything.

And deep down inside, when I drown at the bottom of the abyss, I know that. That's what the voice deep down in the dark blames me for the most. It's a lesson I'll never forget again, it's a foundation that I'll build a stronger me upon.

It's August 2018. A beautiful white dog lies on the rug, at peace at last. It's the last kindness you can do for man's best friend. It's the right thing to do. Simply selfishly it's one of the worst right things I've ever done. The loss of this unconditionally loving best friend brings so much else in to focus. We've known this day was inevitable for a while, she's had a fantastic life. But it's too soon, I want more time with her, we've more adventures to have.

It's January 2010, that first night after. I want more time with her. It's too soon, we've more to say, adventures to share, this can't be the end. I didn't know I could hurt this much.

It's September 2016. The surgeon asks me to sign the consent form one more time, tells me how I won't climb again, how I might well walk with a stick for the rest of my life. It's too soon, I want more time, this can't be how I end.

It's May 2000. We've just stood in front of the preacher and said yes. I've known since the day I met her. We've loads of time. We've so many adventures to have.

It's December 2018. A beautiful puppy called Missy, a puppy I wasn't sure I could love, is asleep on my chest. We're going to be the very best of pals. We've so many adventures waiting to be found.

It's September 2019. I'm back from a successful season working in the Alps. Out in the Lake District, little Missy is atop her tenth Wainwright, I can hear Pushka's song on the wind, I feel Mum's love in the rays of the summer sun. I'm full of possibilities with my bride of nearly 20 years by my side. This moment right now is the adventure.

It's then, now, before and after. It's the good days, it's the days to come. I'm sat in a hollow in the mountains, warm in the light of a glorious day. Today it doesn't matter if it's Glaramara, the Domes du Miage or Quandary Peak. I'm paused but present, fully in the moment. I sit and bring all of me to now. I do this often when I'm alone in the high places. Pause. Sit. Connect. Stretch out the tendons, contract the ligaments. Breathe in the good, let go the bad. Relax into right now. Feel down into the rock, into the earth. Simply be. I do this on the bad days, but just as importantly I also do it on the good days. I do it when I hear laughter on the wind, I do it when I sense I could fall lost in time again. I focus on the connections that ground me to now.

But this isn't the whole or even close to the soul of being mindful. I've slowly learned to reach further, to connect with myself. To find my place right now here on the Earth, to acknowledge my role in the whole of it all, how small I am, how central I am. I can feel the crystals in the volcanic rock beneath my fingers. I can celebrate the parts of my hands with sensation, acknowledge the parts where there's an absence. There's almost a tangible taste to the air, birds sing on the wing, somewhere close by a beck tumbles. The sun on my back seems to expand the range of my senses. I can connect with the natural world, marvel at the majesty, feel it's enduring lack of judgement, appreciate its acceptance of all things. I breathe in slowly, breathe out along the length of my aches, focus on all of it and slowly none of it, drop the pain and worry and doubt one by one.

And then my ghosts come forth.

Kazakh climber Anatoli Boukereev wrote: "Mountains are not stadiums where I satisfy my ambition to achieve, they are cathedrals where I practice my religion." At peace here in that same cathedral, I'll often find myself deep in gentle conversation. It's entirely possible I talk more with Mum now than any other time in the last two decades. Words whispered, written, ushered forth—a recognition of all that was, all that continues to be. I'll tell her of my aches and pains, she'll laugh and tell me to count my blessings. I'll maybe speak of loss, she'll remind me I'm still here in the wonder and speak of love. I'll tell her how sometimes life weighs heavy and I feel older than my years, Nan will interrupt to remind me of the losses old age can really take from you. I'll often laugh at myself and I'm never alone in that, Uncle T will sit in the shade and chuckle with a glorious glee at the humour of it all. Somewhere a beautiful white dog runs free and sings the song of her kind. As I absorb these mountain moments I'll think of wonderful friends I can share them with and give thanks for the chance I have to make that a possibility.

I reach down into myself, I take the time to feel peace at simply being. Breathing slows, the sun warms my skin, I make the specific effort to give thanks. I know that I carry all of them in my heart, timeless within me. Their love lifts my eyes from in to out, from then and maybe to now and yes, to a future that beckons me on. I settle down into the earth, the solid rock supports me, distant ridges fade away rich with the promise of future adventure and I know I've found my own place to be here in these high hills. We talk for a while and I listen, really listen. I'm not alone in this, I never really was. I'm not in pain, I feel stronger than in a decade. I can physically feel the light filling me, I'm not afraid of the dark anymore.

It's called talking therapy for a reason.

Chapter 5

Learning to fly

It's 1974, and I'm a little boy thrown violently against a wall by an angry man. Four-year-old me has made the 'mistake' of telling my new stepfather that his terrifying mother isn't my Nan. With the certainty of any child, I know I've already got two Nans. There's a spasm of violence; I can sense his rage even if I can't name it yet. I don't remember fingers gripping my arm or the pull in my shoulder as I'm lifted off the ground. Fortunately, that pain has been long forgotten—nearly all memory of it lost to time except the buried scars that shape so much of what's to come. Suddenly, I'm flying, free, if only for a moment. It's the first of many traumatic experiences I've spent a lifetime trying to walk away from, to forget, if not forgive.

Fast forward to 2016, and I'm sitting in the ophthalmic department of the hospital. I've been having terrible headaches, and a recent visit to the optician has detected a shadow on the back of my eye. The consultant reassures me that he doesn't think this is related to the headaches. He asks about car crashes or major trauma, and when I reply "no," he tells me the other major cause of this sort of scarring could be shaken or abused child syndrome.

Just like that, I'm thrown back through time, back to that unfathomable moment. Suddenly, a host of ghosts are there in the room with me: a defiant boy, a frightened mother, distant grandparents, a system that failed so many.

That's my earliest childhood memory. Scars aren't always visible; some wounds bleed long after they seem to have healed. For years, I told people my earliest memory was being brought home by a policeman in his turquoise Ford Anglia when I was three. I believed it was true, but now I know it was a lie, a story crafted to prove someone else's point. I've seen that picture countless times: the tall policeman in that iconic hat holding my hand, my mum looking so young and happy. But what I thought it signified isn't real; my experience of it is distorted. Show any small child that picture, and I promise none will tell you the car is turquoise. That's a word from the world of grown-ups.

Being coached to tell other people's versions of events—some truths twisted, others simply fabricated—was an ever-present manipulation throughout my early years, a form of insidious psychological control with lasting ramifications. We teach children the meaning of truth, but what happens when that truth is a lie? From an early age, my truth was often stolen, distorted. I was complicit in hiding my own abuse. When your truth is taken or altered, you lose a part of yourself. You begin to lose a connection to the world that most people take for granted. Even today, I occasionally meet people from that distant past who remember things very differently from me. They're either righteously wrong or saddened by revelation. I'll tell a distant relative something, and they'll smile in a way I've come to know, and another piece of my past dies. So much of my personal history found to be fabricated, false; future falls.

But I do remember that day in 1974. It's taken the fire of the last decade to know I really remember it that I've found an authentic memory, a prophetic precursor of what was to come.

Little did I know it was also the moment that would shape how I might survive, informing my understanding of how I made it to here and helping me redefine my sense of self. I remember flying, launched in a fit of rage that would become all too familiar. It's that moment of betwixt that illuminates the truth. I don't remember hitting the wall or what happened next. I'm sure my mum wasn't there; this early on, I want to believe she wasn't already used to this, not broken down by it yet. I can't recall the angry words, but I remember flying—the sensation of weightless unknowing, being out of sync with the world, just for a moment.

Even as a child, I sensed the significance of that moment, that feeling. It's an escape, a refuge, a way to be somewhere else, to be someone else—surviving in the not-now, safe while it lasts. It's taken a lifetime to understand that the moment of betwixt offers a chance to change an outcome that often seems inevitable.

Counsellors and safeguarding social workers often ask you to recall feelings about specific events; emotional memory resides deep in our old animal brain, it's hard to fake. We all use different words to explain our individual interpretations of the same events. We remember life through personal distortions of time and perspective, but the emotions always linger, even if we learn to look through a prism of our own reflection. I can't tell you the angry words, but I can still feel the anger heavy in the air, that moment before the thunder heralds a storm. I can feel the fury flash into being, sharp like lightning. I don't remember the physical pain; I don't know how badly it hurt. I absolutely know I was scared. I also know it wasn't the last time. But it's the first one I really remember, hidden for a long time, locked in another box and buried.

I was manipulated about the policeman to make a point, perhaps to score points. The intended narrative was that I was safer with my stepfather—that my paternal grandparents were a risk. But of course it was my stepfather who threw me, who kicked me, who would go on to terrorise me for the rest of my childhood, ruining those formative years. That's just one way abusers control people; they make you believe their chosen reality. They take your truth and force you to say their words. I had social workers, family services, and even a child psychologist spend time with me, but fear is a great teacher. I repeated my lines, said them with conviction, and cried myself to sleep—an unconscious collaborator in sealing my fate.

In the decade after she left my stepfather, as Mum and I slowly grew close again, she revealed how it had been for her. I realised my mother had been subjected to that same psychological abuse, that loss of self. We call it gaslighting now: we shouldn't, it's psychological abuse that erodes your sense of self as much as punches or slaps. Painfully, I learned that sometimes she let me take a beating because she wasn't strong enough to stop him.

Latter-life me is confounded that I couldn't see that back then. But when your arms are over your head, as you curl into a little ball, the world becomes a very small place. I'd give anything to have the chance to slip through time and swap places with her now, for this bigger version of me to do better than that lost little me. I'd give anything for one last chance to have any of the men in my mother's life try to put their hands on either of us again.

Decades later, I can appreciate that a life with my grandparents filled with love and safety might seem ideal. But would that path have led me here? Would a terrified child ever find the strength to leave all he'd ever known, to leave his mother, sister, and later a brother behind? I didn't find the strength to leave for years, yet somehow I found the strength to survive staying. I think I learned it in those moments of flight.

Was my stepfather just misguided? Was parenting too difficult? Should he have had to raise another man's child as his own? Can you excuse the inexcusable? Choices. In the 1970s in

England, kids got smacked when they did wrong; it was the norm. I can understand how physical punishment was accepted, but I don't remember being smacked; I remember being thrown, punched, slammed in doors, kicked, and beaten. I can't tell you exactly when as I remember that from all of my childhood. The fear I lived in wasn't how any child should be raised.

In this latter life I've slowly let more memories leak out of the strong little boxes that a little boy built and buried; Sat typing this I'll stop every so often and, in an unconsciously automatic way massage my sore fingers, fingers that aren't quite straight, where they didn't heal just so. I can remember telling the social worker how I broke them—in the doors at school. I'd tell schoolteachers I'd broken them at Scouts, tell Scouts it was football club, and so on, webs spun so naturally I believed them all. I'd guess my stepfather believed I broke them myself, certainly more so as I got older. I broke them with my stubbornness. Holding out, refusing to say sorry for some perceived wrong, refusing to say I'd done whatever it was that had annoyed him no matter how hard he bent my fingers back, how many times he slammed the drawer on my hand, no matter how much it hurt, until it hurt too much and he'd won, got what he wanted, till he'd proven he was the biggest man in the house again. Till he'd proven in his house it was his rules and that, unwanted as I was, that I was lucky he put up with me. Of course that was when he wanted to prove a point. Sometimes he just wanted to hurt you, blame you, take away any happiness you might be hiding. But he'd always make you say sorry, make you say the words, make sure you knew it was your fault, that you'd made this happen. Choices. Right. Wrong.

For most of my adult life loved ones, friends and strangers have all commented on how almost pathologically I don't say sorry. I'll do everything I can to right a wrong, I'll go all out to make amends. I just really struggle to say the word. It's not an excuse; I should do better. But it hurts. Sorry.

In looking back, I've come to question so much. I've always been told that the burns to my hands happened at my grandparents' farm. But my grandparents swaddled me in love. I've known the farm all my life; it's always been my surest safe place. "Farm" is the four-letter word that I think spells "home." Would I, could I, feel that way about a place if something bad enough to damage my hands for life had happened there? I'll never know, but it doesn't fit into the pattern I've found flowing through the rest of those years. Those sensory experiences that hold true for everything else just don't; I have no sense of anything other than safe when I think of the farm. I have no sense of home when I think of anywhere else from those formative years. Maybe a good psychoanalyst could tease out a deeper long-lost truth, but some things... some things really are best left buried in time.

I could write so much about those falls, about the terrible men my mother loved, the men who didn't deserve that love. About the life lessons they taught me then and now.

But I'm not going to, because the honest truth is none of them are worth the effort of recollection. Instead, I'm going to tell you how I think I learned to fly.

There's a picture of me as a child. It's strange, but there were so few. For the longest time, there just weren't pictures of me. This was odd, as my stepfather fancied himself a photographer; he had all the kit, just very limited ideas. Sure, every year the extended family would get a heavily staged Christmas shot, but there were none of me in the events of life you'll find in other family albums. Mum's parting gift changed a lot of that—a gift of memories and moments, many of them not good, but at least mine.

But there's a picture of me as a child. One I saw often when I was happiest. It's my most favourite picture because for so long it was the memory I turned to when I closed my eyes tight and tried to hide, the image that proved to a little boy that flying was indeed possible. Whenever I've seen it, I've always been struck by the smiles; decades wiser, I now see in that little boy and the great big man, the genesis of who I am today. Before I knew any words of meaning, it was the picture that taught me the spell of belief.

There's a beautiful little boy. Dressed smartly, no bruises to be seen anywhere. A little boy holding his grandfather's huge hand. And what a man! What a grin! Happiness shines out of the picture in Kodachrome magic. Two generations apart, they look so much alike, they look so happy together. Some things are just right. That picture had pride of place on the bookcase at the farm. Happiness flows both ways; it spans time. Whenever I see that picture, I'm both then and now, both more and less.

There's a beautiful little boy. Curled up on a dirty stone floor outside in the old coal store. Arms wrapped tight around his tucked in head, knees drawn up: an instinctive defensive posture to try and stop the blows hitting vital organs he's not yet old enough to name. He's screaming into the crook of his arm. Long after it's over and he's locked there in the cold darkness, he sobs until he's empty. Alone in the dark, he begins to fly unconsciously. Out into the future, even if he can't yet frame it, even if he thinks he's retreating back into the past, he flies forward by looking back. He feels that big, safe hand holding his, the giant warm man who smells of love lifting him up, taking him away to safety and happiness. He can't count that many days; he doesn't yet understand a calendar, but he knows he'll be safe again because his grandfather told him so.

The wings that teach him to fly have a name when you get older; the boy lying on the floor can't yet reference it. Hope is the word a little boy doesn't yet know. But even without words, in the invisible language of life, remembered love teaches him to hope. It tells him in the dark that there are good times ahead, validating that future promise with the warm recollection of past love. One tells the tale of the other. When you're alone in the dark with no idea how to pick yourself up or any chance of escape, hope is the most precious thing in the world.

As I became "more trouble than I was worth," I got sent away more often. My grandparents would have taken me for good; they'd tried more than once. The first time they tried to keep me, I was taken back to my mother in a turquoise police Ford Anglia. I don't really remember it, but I've seen the photo. I do remember standing in so many phone boxes—having to find phone boxes not near anyone we knew, where I couldn't be seen, and calling my Nan reverse charges. She'd always ask me questions, then she'd put Granddad Fred on the phone, and he'd just talk to me. I could have listened forever. My grandparents were vigilant; they tried, but 1970s England was a different world. Social Services didn't take little boys away from middle-class insurance salesmen with talking Austin Maestros parked on the drive of suburban semis. Bad things just didn't happen in nice families like those. But that vigilance bought me extra weeks of escape. I couldn't be sent away with bruises or broken bones, and so I knew. I knew escape was coming. Other people would call it a holiday or a visit—but it was an escape. And knowing it was coming was the realisation of those flights.

I learned to physically fly in later life. For nearly a decade, I flew paragliders—huge material sails that fill with air and soar the invisible winds. It's a fickle pastime in the UK, so many factors at play, so many journeys chasing what couldn't be seen. But one thing held true: those moments when the wing lifted you, when you were suddenly free of the burden of gravity, when your possibilities seemed endless—they made the waiting, the chasing, the days of missing out, and the days of staring out the window all seem fleetingly worthwhile. They fed the habit just enough to keep you going till you could fly again.

There's no part of physically flying that makes sense. Sure, I was almost awake in physics class. I've read the books and seen the diagrams. I can tell you all about dynamic buoyancy: how the mass of the plane must equal the mass of the air displaced by the wings for it to fly, but it doesn't really make sense. Quite possibly our inherent fear of flying belies our instinctual knowledge. I think it's quite possible planes, much like people, fly by the power of belief. If it was hope powered by love that first taught me to fly, as I grew, it became self-belief that made it possible.

I've heard I was a stubborn child. I was often told I was difficult, obstinate, annoying, trouble. From an early age, I got back up when I was knocked down. At first, it must have been the urge to run. Later, I recognised the pattern enough to know I stood a better chance on my feet. Even later, I knew it was the only victory I could find; I needed something of my own to hang onto. I didn't know then what I can rationalise now, but my urge to answer back, to be heard—especially close to the end of living at home as the violence escalated, surely reflected my understanding that I had to find a way for my own choices to be made. If someone dominates you physically, it's a hard win to find. If someone dominates you psychologically, it can be nearly impossible. You have to protect the spark that is you with everything.

Stubborn. Difficult. Obstinate. Annoying. Trouble. All other people's words.

I think I was resilient. I slowly learned I could survive, and I kept my belief in myself alive. There are whole books devoted to the development of resilience; every one of them is worth reading. The inspirational Outward Bound Trust was formed during a nation's darkest hour specifically to engender it into future generations. If I could give any one thing to the young people that pass through our care, it would be resilience: the gift of flight.

Head down, physically and metaphorically, it's easier to collapse in than to escape out. I spend as little time as possible in the house: Scouts, football, just hanging out at the bus shelter. I've not begun to rock climb yet, but I have learned how to climb out of a third-floor window. I'm 15 and already a regular at half the pubs in town. Escapism in every sense.

I'm 15, the violence is getting worse at home, and we're moving towards a final reckoning. I'm 15, and I'm starting to think it's him or me. One of us won't walk away from this soon. I'm about 5'4" and 125lbs. My stepfather is a foot taller and nearly twice my weight. I'm 15, and I'm contemplating what it'll take to put him on the floor, to keep him down for good. I'm 15 and researching how much rat poison will kill a man. I know where all the things I can use as a weapon next time are located in every room of the house; I know because I put a lot of them there. No 15-year-old child should ever have to think that way. I've been thinking about it for years.

I'm on the floor of the pantry in our latest house, a faded between-the-wars terrace. It's a typical pantry, deep and narrow, with the fridge at my back. I'm curled up, stacked shelves to each side. It makes it harder for him to get any real momentum, kicks and punches can't reach me with any force. The door misses me; it's a good place to try and avoid a beating. It's the last time he's putting his fucking hands on me ever again.

A week later, I'll put him on the floor with a glass telephone table and leave for good.

It'll take me another decade to understand that there's a reason my Mum never seemed to stop him—that I didn't see what he did to her when she did. Green may have killed her, but my birth father and then my stepfather made her believe men had the right to treat her like that. Abuse is a cycle that's almost impossible to break.

I'd never liked anything as much in my life as I did climbing from the very first moment I tried it. Suddenly, consequence seemed in my control; it was an escapist epiphany, both filling and emptying me at the same time. Years of unknowingly practicing the unacknowledged rituals of flying suddenly found a physical manifestation of their purpose. Emptying my mind of noise, worries, and hurts; distraction through focus; the euphoric high of overcoming a seemingly insurmountable adversity; the literal progression from there and then to here and now.

Of course, I can reflect on this with the wisdom of decades, wrapping it in 21st-century concepts like mindfulness, but back then, I was simply honing the skills I would need to survive later events. I thought I was playing, finally free. A good climbing coach should tell you about purposeful practice, developing muscle memory to perform perfectly. An exceptional coach might explain that the same principle works with your internal processes. Visualisation, focus, centring—all skills that need to be put to good use and mastered. All skills I'd unknowingly been developing during the years I thought I was simply surviving.

Until I found myself paused mid-air, internally still for a moment while rushing toward consequence. I didn't think I could or would fall while climbing. Not when it mattered. Invincibly young, foolishly careless, I thought I'd mastered it all. When you walk out of the fire, you think you're a survivor, that you're blessed. I didn't give the scars I was carrying a second thought. I buried them in boxes I thought I could leave behind. We're told that lightning doesn't strike twice. It often does.

I'm on the Bionnassay Ridge. Truth be told, a lot of these big mountains are straightforward: find the lines of weakness, follow the scratches of those who've gone before, move from known point to known point. Endure, repeat, dig deep, and keep going. And now this. It's a ridge; it should be impossible to go wrong. But there are no rocks, no footprints, no reassuring suggestion of what comes next. My partner is twenty metres back, he's my whole safety plan. If I fall left, he jumps right. As plans go, it suddenly seems laughably inadequate. I've no idea what's solid, what's cornice. It's a brilliant white tightrope.

Pause, centre, slow your heart rate. Believe. I'm here now; I need to be there. Pick yourself up. Make a choice. Go.

High on the smooth wall of rock, I know I need to fly. I don't yet understand the philosophy of weightlessness, but I do know how to deal with this. Pause, find myself, relax, bring everything to now. I've nothing you could even laughingly call a handhold; all my weight is on two footholds that owe more to fiction than friction. It's easy to let the idea of quitting make its appeal: it's always easiest to think you can't. The slab is nearly vertical, but that's enough to allow a balanced pause. A fall from here is almost unthinkable, yet I'm starting to think about it. I can see exactly where I'll hit the boulders below.

But I know how to survive this. As I consciously focus on slowing my breathing, I find an inner monologue, a spell to help me fly. That doesn't matter: where you want to be is what matters now. I've survived this before, perhaps not exactly this, but harder, similar, worse, close enough. I know my feet will hold; I know hands can push just as well as they can pull. I'm balanced here; I just have to nail the sequence to balance there. Flex my fingers, drop my heels, breathe, relax into knowing I can do this. Trust the people you care about who are with you today. Trust those who aren't here today. Trust yourself.

But I can fly further. I've not understood this until decades later: I can fly forward. I haven't just reached today by the reminiscence and support of past successes and survival. It was the hope of the days to come that lifted a little boy up off the cold stone floor. It's the ability to see past this to something else. This route isn't my aim; it's not my aspiration. It's the third of five on this slab, and I intend to do them all. I can look right and see the next; this is easier, this is a stepping stone to there, a thing to be survived. I've survived in the past, but I need to believe I can succeed in the future. I need to lose the weight my mind carries. I need to believe that I can do not just this but what comes next. I can make the future one of my choosing. I reach left and climb.

There's one other moment in flying that needs acknowledgment. It's a moment you think you already know—a moment that I often thought demonstrated how strong I'd become, how on top of my game I really was. It's a moment this journey has made me re-evaluate time and time again. My understanding of it has changed many times; it's inevitability, the only continuity. It's the moment you choose. It's the moment you make a choice or someone makes it for you.

There are so many ways it can happen: the moment that pushes you into the betwixt. Running from or to, that long tentative reach, the door slamming shut as you leave a house filled with hate, the moment you curl up on the floor and leave now to hide in the there or then, the moment you pick up the phone to talk to a stranger. So many ways. And of course, alone in the dark, it can often not feel like any sort of choice you made —much more like you've been pushed. Have I jumped through choice or necessity? Is there a difference?

It's taken me a decade of thinking about the moments of life to realise that's not the question; that's not the way to find the truth in those moments. It's a revelation to understand that it doesn't even matter if you chose to jump, were caught unawares by the fall, or even if you were pushed past the point you could hold on. Because when you find yourself in that moment of pause, there are only ever two choices: fall or fly. But without acknowledging the possibility, the potential of that moment, you'll likely be falling before you even think of flying. And I'm back to belief. You have to *believe* you can fly. You've done it before. If you're reading this now, simply by being old enough to read this, you've flown many times. And yes, I'm sure you've also fallen. We all fall. But you can arrest the fall, catch on, hold the moment, not lose the truth of you. We can all fly. Even more amazingly, we have the power within us to help others fly too.

There's a thing about drowning most people don't know. The people who really drown just quietly slip below the waters and vanish. There's no shouting, no flailing arms, no screams for help. The dark, deep waters take hold, and then they're gone: often in plain sight, just not seen. The noisy casualty has the best chance of survival; they've still got energy; they're trying. It's seldom that doing something or even just doing anything to try and save yourself fails. Crushed by the weight of life, unable to move... that's the slow, steady death of the self. Try. Something is almost always better than nothing. Trying is the very start of flying.

We walk through a big, empty, beautiful house. It's been our home for six years, a testament to our success. We hug wistfully, then lock the door and leave one last time. As we walk down the long drive, it's impossible to see; I didn't realise at the time, but imperceptibly, our feet are just off the ground — we've jumped into the possibility of a different, better life, saying goodbye to so much in the hope of finding something more. From here, we'll open the doors of a little mortgage-free cottage on the edge of the village and then drive into town to sign the papers and sell the business that once seemed impossibly important.

We've known since before Mum died that we're not happy. Since her loss, I've begun to fall, and I'm terrified of dragging others down into the dark with me. What once seemed to matter so much—money, prestige, being a boss—I've come to understand has stolen the joy of simply being, the chance to be more. We sign the contracts, life changes again, and we leap into the unknown.

Flying, fuelled by the memories of the past and the hopes for a better future, seems to overlook the here and now. And now, despite what was or might be is, I'm going to discover, everything. If I can use the past to strengthen a version of myself able to endure the reality of now, then surely hope for a better future can do the same. If I can truly believe in something more than what was or might be, can I actually make the present better than this? Learning to find balance in the moments of now will be a lesson I think I learn in the future, sitting on a rock in quiet reflection. But, as with so much, I'm going to discover that its foundations were set in those dark early years.

It will be tempered into resolve long before I ever know its worth and finding it again will give me the strength to look for a way to love life again.

Chapter 6

My Son, the Mountaineer

A hint of laughter in her voice and perhaps just possibly a touch of pride? A misted memory risen from my subconscious, now aglow with promise in the front of my mind, a possible lifeline for my shattered sense of self, offering the chance of a redemption I can't yet fathom, but one that I'm coming to realise I desperately need to find.

I don't know when I first heard these words; I can't picture the scene or tell you who was there. Were we alone? In a group? Talking? Joking? Truthfully I don't know. But when I close my eyes and look for any hope of a different reality in the dark haunting hours, when I try to hear something other than the voices of recrimination and regret, I can ever so faintly, but oh so clearly, recall these words. They whisper to me, taunt me, lift me and crush me. They were never true. Certainly never when she was with us, never during the times now lost when I think they were spoken. It was just a simple misunderstanding, a failure on my part to explain the difference between climber, crag, mountain and mountaineer. And even that's not all of the truth they carry. Perhaps I liked this mental image Mum had of what I did, I liked it that she had an illusion of the grand, she saw more in it than I did, that maybe it made her proud that I conquered one of her greatest fears. With the freedom that authorship allows I've come to understand this might just, possibly, hopefully, be how my mum saw me, more than I thought I was, something other than broken, the potential all of who I could be. Would that be such an oddity, a mum proud of her little boy? That I don't truly know casts another shadow into the faded past of that lost boy and wistful doubts into the future of the man I might one day hope to be again. It says everything more eloquently than I ever could about so many of the things we never spoke of.

But can these remembered words of yesterday say anything about the hope of tomorrow?

Because now they are words that are coming to define me, shaping me into the carefully crafted image of the son I hope she thought I would be. They have become words I want to define me, a phrase my mind has latched on to in the belief they might be words that show me how. They're the softly spoken spell I'm trying to weave into reality with risk and reward.

I've been, could be, perhaps should be, so many other things.

Son, Husband, Friend, Boss...drunk, funny, angry, broken... there are so many words to label and define, but now I'm truly lost and find myself caught fast by another terrible refrain. In failing as a son, all the other words that should mean so much more seem only to highlight my fall—and I in turn seem to hide from them in shame. If I couldn't do what any son ought to do then how can I claim any of those other names with any sort of honesty, when will the people who say them come to realise I might fail them too? Only these four words seem to offer a way to be something different, a maybe-able-to-love-life-again me. Only these four words seem to hold any power against all the other words that fill my dark hours.

They're words heard through the fog of memory. An almost remembered recollection of a familiar conversation, the soft voice heard through the door before you enter a room. They're the dreaming words that fade behind my eyes as I wake, they speak of a hope of better days to come as I sleep. They've become the words that shape a memory I'm not even sure is real. A memory that I've made real, something to believe in again.

If these are, as I've clearly chosen to believe, the words my mum used to describe a happy me that she was proud of—then perhaps they are words that could make me happy again, make me proud of who I am, turn my eyes from the past to the future. When you're drowning you clutch at anything that might just be enough. A new different me doesn't sound like such a bad hope.

And there it is again, seen with hindsighted eyes, such an obvious dichotomy: it's not a new me. By the time Mum died I had a mountaineering CV that got me into the Alpine Club, I'd climbed some of the hardest rock routes in the UK, I could hold my own on steep ice, I'd summited on three continents. But all that was lost to me then. When I began to fall, my connection to that version of me simply disappeared from cognitive view. When Mum died I was forty and fat, a life of mesmerising moments given over to a life comfortably numb in the pursuit of the socially desirable capitalist dream. Business was booming but my soul was dying.

Falling, everything I thought I was, gone. The sense of deserving what was to come.

And then, though I knew it not, nor for the first time, remembered words of love saved me. A chance clutched—just enough of the climber left in me to aspire to find a way up and out of the dark, just enough resilience left to be able to still believe in flying. Surrounded by love old and new, too blind to see it, lucky enough for it to be unconditional.

At first trips out to the hills were just escapism, friends doing their bit to try and lift my gloom, to distract me from myself. Away from the desk, away from sitting in the dark, away from the temptation of booze and fights with strangers, just away. The endeavour of doing, not needing to talk, separated by 150 feet of rope—not just out into the great outdoors but out of myself both physically and mentally for a while. Much like the sleep that still eluded me, the restorative power of not being internalised, of not circling the deep dark hole for a while, it worked on me slowly but surely, though I didn't see it at the time. More future found wisdom.

Living on the edge of the UK's Lake District the hills are never far away and the rock of the Peak District or the snow of Scotland are all a relatively easy drive, so off I'd go when I could feel the pressure building. Often as not, friends couldn't just drop things and often as often I was really seeking the emotional safety of solitude, still too afraid of which me might be heading out. So off I'd go alone.

Parking somewhere wild. Boots on, probably just a bottle of water and waterproofs, reliant simply on strength and perseverance, not a care for consequence, heading up and away, walking till it hurt, walking till I felt something other than anger and guilt. Looking for the steepest routes, hands on rock, feeling my way to slowly finding that version of me again, losing flab and fear, hoping to shape myself into someone else. But of course physical change was easy. The hardest climbs are always about the head game.

I think I might always have known, but I certainly came to believe the mountains were where I'd find my salvation—it was just the how of that finding I couldn't grasp for the longest time. Again I was looking for easy answers to an almost unfathomable problem.

I don't know when I started to take more risks. Perhaps it was as the stress of the Chancery court built, perhaps it was as I started to hear that other more critical denominator in my own head. But as my internalised stigma and self-loathing built, as I disliked myself more and more, slowly the risks I chose to take grew. Big long walks alone in the hills became steep grade 3 scrambles alone became delicate climbs laced with consequence. And then my eyes and aspirations turned to even bigger hills.

I can say it now but like any addict I hid it at the time—when I was most scared, closest to the edge, risking it all, I felt burningly alive, a sensation strong enough to blaze through the dark, to take all of my focus into the moment. I felt like me again.

An unknown point in time early in that lost decade, 2013 maybe 2014; I've come to walk at a favourite place, a haunt of my youth, somewhere I know the magic of old memories lingers. At least that's the lie I've told myself and worse, that's what I've told those I love. But this is from the time right at the bottom of the abyss. I've no understanding of how bad that is back then, which makes it cut all the deeper now. I've brought rock shoes out of sentimentality. Never much of a boulderer, but perhaps I'll try.

It's been a bad week, I've felt a building anxiety adding pressure and weight to the depression, forcing me deeper into the dark, deeper into myself. Yet another cancelled court date, long conversations with my barrister where he explains to me that he has to advise my mother's murderer on matters of law and it's chargeable to me. He's refused to instruct his own counsel so that he can have days out of his cell. Incredulously we can't rely upon knowledge of the law that he doesn't have, so my poor barrister is having to walk him through the process – a process that is seemingly never going to end. And then he has to tell me about it, and like putting my hand into the fire I have to hear it, I can't turn away. It always begins by being about the case but it always descends to lies and malice. It feels inescapable, like I've put the noose around my own neck. I'm drowning in plain sight. It makes me want to scream, to punch walls. But I think I'm better than that. I think I've a better way of coping.

Feet follow an old remembered route along the crags upper edge until it's possible to scramble down and walk along the base of the crag. Past so many struggles of yesteryear, so many places where we lazed in the sun egging each other onward and upward, waiting for our own moment on the sharp end. I like it here, it's one of those special places that just feels right.

I've been climbing a lot recently, training at the wall with friends, strangers and alone, no real plans, just happy to be lost a while in the meditation of movement—another resurrected version of me that I like so much more than the shell of me that wanders absent in the world most other days.

No real plans. That's a lie. I want to find my very own subtle knife and slice back through time to that long-ago me full of promise, the me from way before but long enough after that hadn't a care in the world. I've not yet started to talk, and these words are unformed pixels immaterial in the ether, but I know I've always been able to focus all of me into a climb, I've always been able to find that calm centre. And I desperately need the quiet now, I need a reprieve from myself.

There are so many other ways to do this… but I don't know them yet, or at least I've lost any sight of them in the dark. This seems the only way I can find any relief.

Whatever I've told myself or others I've always been coming to climb—even if I've genuinely not known that all the way here. It feels good to stand at the foot of the crag and feel small. There's a couple of guys down by the last chequered buttress but I don't want to go that far; I've always loved the honesty of these climbs on the steep slabs, and for now they're all mine. A perfect smooth wall of rock, with consequences piled high in the shape of age worn boulders at their base, technically not that hard, psychologically nails. I play a while traversing, I follow a couple of the easy lines to the top just to feel the sense of height, be happy with moving upwards. I don't know if I feel it then or add it now in recollection, but there's a building sense of an itch that needs to be scratched, an undercurrent that warns of the possibilities of not focusing, I can feel a considerable part of me isn't here, is still railing with an angry internal dialogue, still looking inwardly down rather than out and up.

The first couple of moves are so polished now. Even back in the day they were slippy; every climber who's ever stood here has tried these moves. It's easiest to pull through them quickly till you're higher than even the tallest hopeful's reach; step left above the boulders and now you can balance. It's been two decades since I was here but my body still remembers the sequence, still remembers how all those little ledges are going to be just not quite as good as you want them to be, how the tantalising combination of friction and nearly draws you on intoxicatingly upwards, hands really for balance, weight flowing across and over, pushing up and into equilibrium, trying to centre your gravity somewhere just inside the rock, risk increasing incrementally the higher you go, flow becoming more important than holding. It commands all of my attention at a level little else can, senses alive to every input, messages from each fingertip and every other part of my hands, nuances full of meaning in every foothold fire along my nerves. I'm reading the rock with my eyes, looking hard for the imperceptible imperfections that will make all the difference, I can taste the adrenaline in my blood, the only discernible sound is the peaceful mantra of my breathing.

It's all done in 40 moves or so. Just as consequence threatens to overwhelm it's over, a strong pull on comparative jugs finds you on the top of the crag. Less than five minutes have passed in the here-and-now world. But in the internal world, a lifetime seems to have paused. The absence of anything other than the climb, the surge of suddenly being so very alive washing so much toxicity out of my psyche I feel reborn… for the shortest of whiles. But the respite has been enough to gather my resolve, to know I can face the fight some more, to know the old me who might one day be the future me is still alive somewhere inside. I sit a long while atop the crag, reliving the moments just been that connect me to so many other memories of survival and ecstasy, happier times, stronger times.

Now I'm in the Alps for six weeks. The first week is with Cat. She's never been before and I know she's apprehensive about what to expect. Our aim is for some mid-level mountain walks which we do, and wonderfully I can see her falling in love with the place, the mountains, the valley, the views, the atmosphere.

The drive to Chamonix, as anyone who's ever done it will confirm, is truly dull—until the last hour when suddenly mountains rise in front of you, the road takes a crazy rise on stilts and you wind your way into the valley itself. I've done this drive half a dozen times in the last two years now, but this is the first time I've done it with someone whose face I want to see. As we pass the Christ on the hill at Les Houches I see Cat's face light up, she strains to look upwards through the van's windows —but unlike the mountains she's used to back home these ones keep stretching upwards—from the valley floor it's just not possible to see the tops. I know the tall snow-covered mountains seem impossible, full of taken risks I can't yet admit to, so I'm keen to point out the trails in the woods, the just discernible lines of the

Grand Balcons and, as we drive towards the apartment we've rented in Argentiere, we get a glimpse of the famous little red train making its improbable way up to the Mer de Glace.

It's also the first time I'll be alone here, if I ever really am alone anymore.

When Cat leaves I'm fairly forlorn, an almost instant homesickness overcomes me and I want desperately to follow her, to book a flight and make her return; the reality of our separation is far more felt than its anticipation. And yet after so long in the dark I've started to welcome the pains of loss. I need to be here alone. Shamefully I make myself believe that it's better for Cat to have time away from me, but truth be told "shameful" is a word written much later in this telling; at the time I earnestly believe I'm doing the right thing. Big boys don't cry. Alone I know that I'll find the time to think about the reasons and motivations that have made me make versions of this trip so many times. I know that this time will in no small part be spent thinking of Mum, thinking of how I've changed not just my, but our lives. I've started to build a mental self-image, I've the visualisation of a journey I'm only halfway along, that I don't know I can finish. But is it real? Is it a worthwhile reality? This is something that I know I must find my own answer to. Future me reads this and laughs out loud. That I thought I was halfway already, that I thought the real journey had even begun.

I've plans to meet up with various people over the coming weeks. I've also plans to spend a lot of time alone. I'm still not sure how well I'll be able to play with others—or which me the mountains will find.

We head to Zermatt based on a better forecast. Despite having heard such reports of its beauty the initial impressions are so overwhelmingly awful that I want to turn tail and drive the 3 hours back to the comforting familiarity of the Cham valley. In its drive to banish cars and be beautiful the staging post of Täsch has been created, an abhorrence in these alpine meadows, testament to human contradiction. We park and try to see past hundreds of cars, cold grey concrete and the ravages of man to the Breithorn and beyond.

The mountains here aren't green and rich in colour like the Alps I've just left, more these dramatic shapes show the scars of the processes that created them, and also the scars of the processes that enjoy them. True the Matterhorn looms overall in a majestic manner; but I have seen the pictures before and, perhaps still depressed at the predictable commercialisation of Zermatt, I'm less impressed than I hoped for.

We take the Kliene Matterhorn lift to 3,820 metres. The weeks I've already done up high mean I'm well acclimatised. We kit up efficiently and stride out with purpose, by the first incline we're overtaking people. We make a strong team. The main crocodile of climbers turn away from us to bag the simple version of the Breithorn, a couple of hours plodding and a 4,000—metre summit is theirs. We have more ambitious mountaineering aspirations. We continue on, heading for the col at the end of the Briethorn's impressive ridge, our plan to bag Castor and Pollux then bivvy at the Rossi Volante Hut (3,850m), gaining a valuable night's acclimatisation before returning by the traverse of the full Breithorn ridge.

As we slowly make progress our attention is taken by the darkening clouds to the East and the plumes of snow violently blowing from the ridge. Already the crocodile has turned tail; very few parties can be seen still heading up. Protected somewhat by the mass of the mountain we continue onwards, it's exhausting but the steady pace and rhythm mean we make good progress. We swing the leads: B is younger than me but he's a strong climber and already has lots of experience in this terrain. As I lead out across the crevasses, B is my safety much as I am his. I'm mentally if not physically tired. But it's too early in this telling to have yet found the wisdom to acknowledge the other weight I'm carrying. I pause, step forward and only then notice the void left and right of me. Then I fall through the soft snow bridge. B falls back, buries his axe perfectly and catches me, just a head sticking out of a crevasse. We both laugh in relief as I snow-swim a ridiculous breaststroke up and out, this has the makings of a good trip. B's summer has been one of disappointment so far, I really want for this good young man to have a high to finish on—and feeling myself acknowledge that for him is another quiet sign of the magic time in the mountains is working on me. The mountains are making more of me, moving my focus from in to out, it feels better to be invested in B than contemplating me. It's a steady slog, the bulk of Castor dominates the view ahead, the Briethorn's long jagged ridge shelters us, but as we near the col we can see that the wind on the tops must be approaching 50mph. Snow flumes sting in our direction and suddenly Castor is covered with parties making their way down fast, all trying for the safety of lower down. We spot the hut, sat on rocks 100 metres above us. We don't make a decision, there is no decision to make. We head for it, it should be a walk, instead it's a fight of the kind we both enjoy.

The next morning we dig our way out to glorious conditions and head to the rocky ridge of Pollux. It was a long cold night listening to the storm hurl chunks of ice and rock at the metal roof but the sun soon warms us and we both climb well, barely pausing at the crux wall, making excellent time, everything back on track. Striding on to the knife thin snow summit the vista ahead is full of promise: the Lyskamms lie waiting, the Dufourspitz dominates, and gendarmes stand everywhere honouring these high places. We pause in quiet contemplation, then laughing we point out other routes. We can see our next peaks, the rest of the adventure stretches before us. Then the wind picks up, distant thunder rolls up from the valley below and just like that this trip is over. We make the last lift down just ahead of the storm. No sign of our old footprints visible as we retrace our route.

The mountains often make your choices for you. I don't yet know that's one of the things I'll come to value most, but future me can see the relief it brings, decisions deferred, an absence of doubt and blame, a forced acceptance. Later me will be able to admit I now know it's not my best me on many of these early trips to the big mountains, but I can also acknowledge that it's so much time spent in the high hills that has drawn that honesty from me. It'll still take me most of a decade to truly appreciate the calm I feel in the reality of my insignificance being made manifest by those visits to these places, longer to understand how that same balance can be found elsewhere, but even then I can tell I feel lighter, free for a while.

After two more weeks of solo climbing, picking up climbing partners from message boards and valley bars, I found myself staring up at the Petite Aiguille Verte. This was meant to be my final moment of freedom—a last grasp at the kind of risk where nothing but my own survival was at stake, easy to accept as I didn't really matter, responsible for naught. There was no one waiting on me, no one relying on me, no need to be anything other than absent. This was my chance to breathe in the thin air without the burden of responsibility, and to clear my mind completely, if only for a few more hours.

I had felt increasingly at home in the higher mountains all season, but it was never about proving myself to them. I didn't need to. I needed to prove myself to myself. The mountains were vast, wonderfully indifferent. And somehow, in that indifference,

I felt free—free from thought, from memory, from the voices in my head. The Petite Aiguille Verte was small by comparison to its towering neighbours, yet still a gateway to that precious emptiness. I could already see their jagged silhouettes in the sky, especially its big brother, the Aiguille Verte, which I'd convinced myself I'd tackle next time, if only so Rébuffat might accept me as a true mountaineer; other people's measures yet again. But I wasn't there for next time. I was there to escape today. I didn't fully realise how desperate I was for it, I was blind to the stupidity of the risks I was taking.

I hadn't even bothered with a detailed plan, just a photo of a guidebook. I started late, ambled onto the glacier as if the whole endeavour were a casual hike. I hadn't checked the forecast properly—just a lazy glance out of the window. I didn't study the route; I'd simply checked how often the lift ran. All I really wanted was to keep moving, to let the exertion push everything else out of my mind. I wasn't thinking, and that was the point. It's astonishing to recall it now, how flippant I was, how arrogantly I approached this mountain. With hindsight, it feels almost like I was daring it to remind me of my place.

The ascent started as nothing more than a pleasant distraction. The climb from the Montets was smooth—just a steady diagonal across the glacier, leading to a steep, short wall of rock that felt more like an annoying obstacle than a challenge. I remember smiling to myself as I tackled the next icy headwall the guidebook warned about. It wasn't even as difficult as the notorious 'bad step' on Crinkle Crags back home —only the stakes were higher, the drop more severe. But it felt easy, and I liked that. I pulled over the top without a second thought, feeling brilliantly alive, as if the simplicity of each movement somehow justified the risk.

Up here, the mountains seemed more honest than life down there in the valley, the wind carrying only the occasional echo of voices from student climbers learning the craft far below, mere black dots against the white expanse. But the silence wasn't comforting—it was consuming. Each footstep carried me further into it, deeper into the quiet void I sought. My mind emptied, each rhythmic step erasing thoughts, worries, fears. I didn't have to think about what had brought me here. I could just be here, in the moment, letting the risk fill the space where my thoughts would have been.

As I moved up the rocky ridge, the glacier far below looked like it belonged to another world. From this height, it was impossible not to feel small, insignificant, like a speck moving across a vast, uncaring landscape. My stomach tightened reflexively at the sight, a reminder of how far down everything was, how one misstep could make it all vanish in an instant. And yet, I pushed those thoughts away, savouring the absence of responsibility, of needing to protect or guide anyone but myself. It was just me and the mountain, and for a while, that was enough.

Then I heard it. The unmistakable, gut-churning crack of rockfall. It was distant at first, a sharp metallic ping that grew into a thunderous crashing, ricocheting off the mountainside. Instinctively, I dove behind an outcrop, heart pounding in my chest. The noise intensified into a roar, and then I saw it—a massive boulder, the size of a fridge, flew past mere feet away and continued tearing its way down the mountain, smashing everything in its path. It obliterated the very route I had just climbed minutes earlier, as if it had singled me out, mocking my cavalier approach.

Far below, I watched as tiny dots scattered, students scrambling to escape the boulder and its cascading entourage's deadly path. I crouched frozen, helpless, watching this monstrous rock fall with horrifying precision down the same line of weakness I had foolishly chosen. It was a brutal reminder of how fragile everything was, how quickly things could go wrong. And in that moment, I realised what I had been risking all along.

I wasn't just risking my safety. I was gambling with the futures of everyone I cared about. There were people waiting for me, trusting me to come home. For the first time, it dawned on me how selfish I had been, thinking only of the escape, the relief of a clear head. I hadn't considered what I stood to lose: the people who would be left behind if I didn't make it back. It wasn't just about surviving this climb. It was about what my absence would mean to them. I risked throwing others into the same sort of darkness I was doing my all to avoid. The thought hit me harder than the rockfall itself.

When I scrambled up to a more solid band of rock, I met G, another climber who had been just as reckless as I was. We didn't need words. His expression said it all. We were both lucky to be alive. We made a hurried plan to descend together, grateful for the rope I hadn't even meant to bring, that I was just carrying for weight. As we picked our way down, we passed crater after crater, the scars left by the rockfall, evidence of what could have been. Each step felt heavier, the realisation of what we had risked pressing down on me with every metre.

By the time we reached the plateau beneath the lift station, the place was deserted. The climbers we'd seen earlier had already gone, no doubt to count their blessings. G and I untied in silence. He didn't look back once as he disappeared into the station, and I didn't blame him. We both knew we had pushed our luck too far, made terrible choices. I stood there for a long time, looking up at the diagonal slash our tracks had left across the snow, at how it was broken by a vivid grey scar of debris and it was impossible to not understand how close my arrogance had taken me to a very different outcome.

I had wanted an empty head, a brief reprieve from thought, from everything. But what I got was a stark reminder of how much I had to lose. The mountains didn't care about my wishes, my need for clarity. They weren't indifferent or merciful. They simply were. And in that moment, I finally understood the real cost of the risks I had been taking. It wasn't just about me anymore. It was about everyone I'd ever loved, everyone who would be left behind. And that was a risk I had no given right to take.

As I descended the lift alone, the weight of that realisation settled on me. This wasn't just a close call—it was the moment I stepped back from the edge, the moment I began to move toward something better. Somehow more responsible, more aware of the true stakes. When I now look back I see me beginning to understand what matters most. I didn't know it at the time but this was the moment I took my first real steps; both back from the edge and forward towards better.

I'm weather-lost in the van. It's been raining torrentially for 18 hours. I've surfed the web, I've read my book. I've done most of the things I can to pass the time, but eventually I'm left to my thoughts. It doesn't take long for the self-questioning voice to appear: "have I been selfish? Has it been worthwhile? Am I better for the experience?" I don't need to dwell on these for too long to know I don't yet have any answers. What I have thought about a lot is who would have to make another terrible call to Cat, to others who love me. About what right I have to put anyone through that, about what it says that I'm thinking of this for the first time now after so many of these trips away.

Taking the call about Mum came so close to breaking me for good—and yet so much of that call was out of my control. I was a passenger on a storm already fully raging. Now I'm making choices in the comparative calm that may well hurl those I love into the void.

The next day the last of my friends from the UK arrive. I smile a lot, we do the tourist thing, I play host and guide. Picnics at high glacial lakes, long lazy rock routes in the sun. We finish with a bivouac on the Dôme du Goûter and sunrise on the summit of Mont Blanc.

It's time to go home and learn to be more than this.

Over the next decade I return to these high mountains time and time again. I still take risks because ultimately that's what climbing is, but I manage that risk, I really do, to the very best of my abilities. I'm not ready to be somebody else's lost love just yet. Eventually we buy a teeny tiny apartment at the foot of Mont Blanc. I can see majesty in every direction. But I'm starting to really understand what it means to come home, what the real win actually is.

I'll go on to tick a dozen more 4000m peaks, but the magic really returns when I slowly I start to climb the mountains I want to, rather than picking at a list I think myself and others might measure me by. I still adore the thrill of going out alone, often to the peaks and obtuse summits I can see from our apartment, many without even a name, but with a special meaning to me. But when I do I go prepared, I leave a plan and joy of joys I can stay in touch in this modern world. Eventually I'll go on to master the wisdom of climbing the mountains other people want to, they somehow often mean so much more. A ghost of a future truth I'll learn to laugh about.

Yet it's the pettiest of things, the most illusory of successes. Yes, it can mean everything in the moment. Yes it's the most emphatically alive sense of being, a conquest of so much more than geographic stature. But ultimately it means so little in the grandest scheme of things. I'd forfeit all those moments to have her back. All that risk, so much so often nearly lost, and I'm only a little wiser.

It's December 2019. I'm in a bar in North Wales, the sound of laughter and happy chatter is everywhere. I'm surrounded by lots of lovely latter-life friends, we're wrapped in the camaraderie of our common passion. They're nearly all people I'd implicitly trust and there's a wonderment which requires more than a moment of appreciation in that alone. Internally I'm smiling that wry smile all to myself, outwardly I'm beaming, glass in hand as people pat me on the back and hand me more drinks. I've just been made the honorary President of the British Association of International Mountain Leaders, having been the Chair of the Board of Directors for the last four years. Now, just as I'm finally realising it doesn't matter one little bit, I've reached another mountaineering summit. Yet more flatteringly descriptive words, another new name, just as I'm coming to understand it's never been what the words say that has mattered most. Somewhere a beautiful lady is looking down and laughing at me; I'm beginning to have an inkling I might just know what she means.

I chased it down, I can only guess driven by my subconscious; it certainly wasn't something I was ever conscious of. The moment I heard in a passing conversation that there were qualifications in mountaineering, that it was possible to earn a living, to live a life in the mountains, I set off. One by one, another list of ticks, and again—eventually it's the other people that come to mean the most. Slowly, surprisingly, I become a high trekking guide and a rock climbing instructor – making memories and passing on skills, helping people find their path, choose their challenges, overcome their fears.

Escapism, reasoning, hiding.

Even if I didn't know it at the time I'd set myself on another path, a more positive direction. Now I wouldn't just escape, play and risk myself in the mountains; now it would be something more, I'd be rooted in the responsibility of others, lifted by the reward found in that. Slowly I'd find a way to give as well as take. In doing so I've received more than I ever imagined possible. It's taken this decade to begin to understand that the mountains gave me the space, let me find the room to allow myself to look outwards again, to open myself to others again, to connect with that happier me from another time. I thought I could hide inside the tiny moments of respite, lose myself in the grandeur of scale, burn bright enough to outshine the dark. I'd forgotten what really matters most.

By every measure that I can find I'm a mountaineer. And heartbreakingly it isn't enough.

I can't ever be the son I needed to be. How do I make a peace with that?

Be the person your mum hoped you'd be.

Has this lifted me enough to see that now?

Time spent in the mountains learning to connect with myself and those I love has shown me once more that I have it within me to survive the dark days, that I know how to fight my way out into the light, but it's also reminded me that there needs to be something more. You can't always run away from a thing, you can't distract yourself for ever – eventually you have to make a peace with it.

Probably the best solo mountaineering day out in the Lake District is Pinnacle Ridge on St Sunday Crag. From home I can be parked in half an hour, at the base of the route an hour later. It's my go-to place when I need some me time. I really couldn't tell you how many times I've climbed it, but I'd guess I'm well into three figures now. It's not always a conscious choice, I'm often in the valley before I'm sure that's where I'm heading. It's probably the best day out—such a subjective statement. It's not especially hard, but it's got enough consequence to require your focus. It's not difficult enough to warrant any real worry, I can meditate in the movement, be at one with the environment. Focused and empty all at once. Distracted just enough to be aware, aware just enough to be distracted.

When Mum was taken I'd not climbed properly in years. Yet it was here I came with my feet following an invisible but familiar way, climbing in search of an old remembered me I could maybe trust as I tried to contemplate the unknown and make sense of so much. I've no idea how long that climb took, but when I passed the eponymous pinnacles I found a sheltered hollow in the rock and sat a long time alone in this wild place trying to fathom a way forward. I sat there trying to be simply a part of the mountain, I felt my core chill, felt my breathing slow, hidden inside until all was still—and then I opened my eyes and tried to see a me-sized anything on the far valley walls. There was a comfort and a realisation in the impossibility of it. There still is. I've returned for nearly every major moment since, the catharsis found in the simplicity of just climbing helping me through the losses of Molly, Tony, Pushka, Nan, Alison and more. It's somewhere I've brought the people that matter most to me in the world, hoped they'd see the me I really am. I didn't know it at the time, or rather I wasn't conscious of it, a lifetime later I'm coming to realise my subconscious may well have always known, something deep in the *id* guiding my way, raising mine eyes unto those hills. The place where that long lost me knew I'd find my salvation.

It's a find-your-own-way sort of a climb; the best kind, no prescriptives. Start at the bottom, make your way to the top. As simple as you could ever hope for life to be. But. It's not. Wander too far left and it's simply a steep walk, no thrill, no truth to be found for me. The odd patch of loose ground waiting to stop you. I've never been a fan of aimless or easy. Stray too far right and you'll find yourself on the side wall of the great gully, dank and dark. A fall from there would be your last. But right here on the edge? Between too little and too much? Well, that's the best line, it's where truth feels sharpest. Choices. Sometimes you need to know. Or maybe you don't. Most times I need to know.

Flowing, I thought this was my best me. In the dark I thought I had to burn oh so brightly.

Glowing, I've come to see this still might be my best me, or at least an important part. It's where I'm happiest. But can I only be happy here at the edge of losing it all? I need to find a way to carry that happiness within me, to be that better me, I need to find a way for it to happen everywhere.

Perhaps my absence from the world, the risks I've taken, perhaps they've been what's brought me to the real understanding: that I'm happiest surrounded by those I love. In the smile of my wife, in the embrace of my friends, the camaraderie of fond acquaintance. I'm happiest besides a wise old dog, a beautiful bouncing puppy. Perhaps I'm happiest there because I've found this touchstone for and of my soul, this momentary me that has seen a glimpse of his own true self.

My son the mountaineer.

So much lost in the translation of need.

It was never my fleeting foolish deeds that put the warmth into those words. It wasn't meaningless achievements she never understood that made her smile.

I wasn't listening with my heart.

My son the mountaineer.

My son who survived.

My son who's making his own way.

My son in his own place.

My son, happy, shining bright.

Words of love.

Chapter 7

Remember me with a smile

A play on words, the words written on Mum's gravestone in the hope they might one day be true. Written at a time when they simply seemed impossible.

By the time we reach adulthood just about all of us will have experienced loss, have been through the process of grief—hopefully emerged on the far side, painfully a little wiser. But how many of us can actually remember the first time they smiled again?

It's been a decade and it's only of late that I'm approaching the last stages of a complex journey out of the darkness of depression, anger, self-hate and recrimination. So close to an ending I can now pause and be thankful that along the way I've learned to recognise the signposts, to slowly spot the path, to find my way back to a life of love and happiness. The transition from mourning what's lost to giving thanks for what was has been a tangled web of regret, guilt and hard-won appreciation, fitfully forged with a determination not to let the dark win. The realisation that looking for a way to live my best life, finding a way to try and somehow be more than I was before, that happiness was the truest and perhaps only real way to honour Mum—that was when I first smiled a wry smile, realised how twisted the path out of the dark would be. A few years after her loss, somewhere as I was floundering, as the protracted farce of the Chancery court kept the wounds vivid and festering, I realised I was further down than I knew and risked being lost for good, I realised I'd maybe just enough left to make one last flight.

I'd taken countless risks to distract myself, ways to try and block out one thing with another, none of them actually aimed at changing the core problem: my deepening, awful sense of self. I'd run the UK's toughest marathons and I knowingly continued to run as the damage to my knees and ankles got worse, by then I *wanted* it to hurt. I scared myself stupid on the side of cliffs, took ridiculous risks in the big hills, wandered alone until my feet were quite literally broken. But the human mind is an odd machine, physical pain just another thing to learn. All these ways of hurting myself slowly became normalised, accepted by the system. Distraction became diluted. Over time, like any addiction, it took more and then more to reach the point I was aiming for, to get to the place where my thoughts were silenced if only for a while. As it became more than I could physically endure, as body and mind started to break down I knew I had to find a way to change the pattern, to change how I saw the world and my place in it, but most of all, to change how I saw myself.

And so I began a conscious journey to try and find the wonder again, to appreciate the moments I knew I was missing, to look for the shining stars I used to believe in.

Some days just opening the curtains was a win, keeping a smile on my face till Cat left for work, before falling back down into the easy embrace of the abyss. Days lost on the couch, absent in the moment, life slipping by. I knew I had to find a new reason, something to help me rise up when the depths beckoned, a way to light my own fire, to find something that might guide me out of the dark. Everyone who's ever been held by the abyss knows this—but doing it, finding a way, even finding the energy to look for a way… that can be almost impossible at times. All those people and memes that tell you to be positive, to just get over it, that a journey of a thousand steps… it's not the first step that's the hardest. I made so many first steps. I picked myself up and set out so many times. So many dead ends, even more abandoned journeys. It's finding a reason to keep going when you stumble, it's the step after you pick yourself up for the umpteenth time, the impossibly hard step forward when all you want to do is fall back. That's the hardest step.

Some things were simply basic life; getting dressed, shaving, making myself look like a functioning person again. Some were about structure, the recognition of just trying with the rituals of being: starting the day with three sun salutations, making Cat's lunch, brewing real coffee instead of instant. Some were physically beneficial: doing my physio exercises, losing weight, going to bed early. As I got further down the path these lists would get longer and more complex. As I started out I can't tell you I did them every day, or most days, or none. It's like that in the dark.

Once the step-by-small-step of these simple basics had gotten me to a point where I could actually face the outside world I went searching for a way to find those magical moments, to try and look for the good again.

I'd read a lot about mood journals, about putting time into every day, but even though they're recommended by just about every therapist ever it simply seemed an impossible task. Most of social media was too much of a veneer, and I was as guilty as anyone—hiding behind those empty happy illusions—but then a friend mentioned Blipfoto[10]. A quirky little photography site. A journaling site for some, just pictures for most. A one-year challenge for many, a life changing interaction for a few. On the 1st of January 2014 I published my first picture and a handful of words, my first journal entry. A tiny part of me given to the ether, an act of looking out rather than in.

I didn't know that I would or could commit to it; I certainly didn't have any understanding of the magic this simple little thing would start to work on me. A decade later I now credit it with being one of the foundations of this new me that I've slowly built. It was one of the subtle ways in which smiling, remembering Mum, remembering Mum with a smile all became possible again. The searching out of an image, the having to go and find something worthy of recording forever, it made me start to look, really look, again. I soon realised that I didn't want to focus on the often overwhelming dark; it was the moments of wonder and beauty that I wanted to make a record of. Falteringly I started to write more, to show a little of my inner self to the world. Word by word I started to write about the good in my day, rather than dwell on the bad. Each entry a tiny, recorded step away from the dark. Well, mostly; there may have been the occasional slip or two. There was also the interacting with strangers, slowly getting to know other people's reality, seeing the moments they chose to share, gentle jokes, softly told tales, bit by bit it all gradually began to change the way I saw the world. What I saw around me became more positive than negative, and slowly, slowly but perceptibly, what I started to notice in the internal world began to change too.

---

[10] https://www.blipfoto.com The platform was nearly lost a few years ago – a CIC buyout by a devoted community of users kept it going – but a lot of early content was sadly lost.

A decade later this record of the moments of my latter life, a journal that maps my walk out of the dark—it's the very real record of how I learned to smile again.

April 9ᵗʰ 2015. Giving Thanks; Celebrating Mum

Today should have been my Mum's 63rd Birthday—oddly, the age at which she'd have retired, done all those things she told us about, but tragically will now never do. It's been five and a bit years since she was killed, a span of time in which everything has changed in the lives of her family—perhaps none more so than I.

Over those five years we've seen and heard things no-one should ever have to. We've all had moments of darkness and times when we've not been able to see the way forward—and from time to time for all of us I'm sure that will always be the case. But now each of us have, to differing degrees, found our own ways to move on with our lives. There are still moments when I reach for the phone to make a call that will never be connected, or think "I must tell Mum"...but I've learned to live with that pain, to shrug my shoulders, grit my teeth, and carry on. The darkness is a heavy weight, but I'm learning to look for the stars.

When we buried Mum we put "Remember me with a Smile" on her gravestone—a play on words for a beautiful smiling lady —written at a time when I wasn't sure it could ever be true. Through the last five years, despite being dragged in and out of the courts with her killer, there have been rare moments when unbidden an image would come to mind. The Mum I knew from my early childhood, the independent lady (we saw from the outside) who came to visit, the laugh that lit up a room, and occasionally I could think of her and smile a sad smile before I reached for the Scotch. It was something at least. A couple of years ago we made a pact not to commemorate the day she died —and, though I didn't know it at the time, for me that was a turning point, the moment when the chance of letting the good and positive take hold again bloomed into being, a chance for our wounds, however vivid the scars, to begin to heal.

For so long mum's name, the thought of her, conversations about her, they were wrapped in upset, anger, horror, guilt...nothing good. To reach a point where we might turn our backs on that, to look past the events of five years ago and see the Mum we should be remembering, the Mum who would tell the world she was proud of me when really she was furious, the Mum who would swear at the ref when my brother played rugby, the Mum who was so looking forward to being the best grandmother in the world, to be able to simply think of Mum and not how she died. This was not such a bad thing to hope for.

After Mum died good friends took me back to the mountains —my wonderful wife insisted I went—I need to acknowledge they all knew me better than I knew myself back then. At first it was the simple exertion, a physical way to empty my mind and escape thoughts and events I'd feared were going to come to define me, but slowly I refound the peace and tranquillity—both externally and vitally, internally—that the mountains bring to me. And even if I didn't know it at the time when I look back now, I can see that it was when the long slow process of healing began. In the mountains or on a rock face there's a real chance to be at one with your surroundings, the universe and whatever else you hold dear. There are moments when every ounce of you must focus down to a grain of sand – and others where you can't help but realise just how tiny you really are in the grand scheme of creation—and in those moments I believe you truly get to glimpse the truth of who you are and can be—for me the mountains offer a chance to find your soul.

In the years after she died we sold our business, moved out of the big fancy house and changed our lives – aware suddenly of the fleeting opportunity that this life is—of the chances lost and those yet to be taken—simply knowing that we wanted to be, and mum had always wanted us to be, happy. I now spend my days (mostly) wandering and climbing in the mountains—returning home to a house full of paintings and the sound of laughter—I'm grateful for what our lives are becoming. Even with clients, but especially when I'm on my own, there are moments of solitude and time for reflection (Mum is often with me in the hills) it's entirely possible that I chat to her more these days than I ever did as an adult. A connection I thought severed and lost has been remade and I'm learning to find a peace in that.

Mum never really got the subtle differences between rock climbing, fell walking or mountaineering—at least that's what I like to think. There may of course have always been a gentle, loving, even prideful mockery in her greeting "ah, my son the mountaineer," but I'd like to think she'd be pleased with the life I'm trying to build now.

Today should have been my Mum's 63rd birthday. Today I climbed a mountain and remembered her. Today I smiled again for the first time in too long.

April 9th 2016. Giving Thanks; never alone

April 9th, Mum's birthday, today she should be 64. For 25 years I refused to work on my birthday, but now it's this date that's blanked out in the diary, today is a day for me and my mum, and today she was most certainly smiling down on me as it was a glorious day to get into the hills.

It's six years now since mum was taken from us and in those years our lives have changed enormously, in many respects for the better, something I know she's happy to see, something I struggle to be able to accept. But this last six months I've been personally beset with injuries and setbacks, stacking up and debilitating me, threatening to steal this second chance at happiness. I think as the months and the injuries have gone on and on, as my mental and physical recovery has seemed harder and harder, I've fallen deeper into the depths than an apparent optimist like me should be able to. When Mum was killed anger, grief and guilt held me for far too long—but even then as I fought to hold them off, to find a way out of the dark, I knew I was falling. Recently I've thought I was happily back in the light; to feel the grip of the darkness take hold again has been far more difficult to come to terms with than I'd ever have thought.

Today I was always heading into the hills, the now ever-present pain not allowed to stop me on this day—so I strapped up the ankle and wrist, took a lot of ibuprofen and set forth good and early. As ever the mountains worked their old slow magic. Each step into the long, lonely valley of Langstrath took me further into the wonder, each handhold lifting me further towards the light. Sat peacefully alone atop a crag, with a 360° panorama and the sun on your face it's difficult not to feel blessed. Returning five years ago to a life in the mountains reinforced some old friendships, but I've also made more new friends in these 'second life' years than in the 20 before: friends who've supported and encouraged me, laughed, and on occasion cried, with me—all of whom I'm immensely thankful for.

On Cam Crag Ridge today I paused before the steep little headwall and realised that whilst this is still a relatively easy day out even now for me, there are many for whom it's just not possible. I smiled wistfully at my old self; it's not the physical exertion or the risk that made today special, it was the appreciation of my place in the scheme of things, the love of the journey as it were. Whilst I'll never get to show this place to my mum she'll always see it through me, I can bring others I love to here and remember those gone. I smiled at my blessings and scrambled to the top.

I've written before that God and I no longer see eye to eye, but that doesn't mean I'm without faith or don't think there could be something more. Today, in a cathedral such as this, who could not? With warm sun on my back, skylarks singing on the wing and stars sparkling in the tumbling becks it's impossible not to believe in something more, not to give thanks for it all.

Sat in a hollow on the flanks of Glaramara this afternoon, looking out and not in, absorbing the majesty of the fells I read these words back and realised I'd written *we* instead of *I* in many places. Today was one of the good days, today Mum was most certainly with me and today we were both smiling.

April 9th 2018. Giving Thanks; the love of strong women

I'd given up my hollow hope of being in the hills today—the day I observe my remembrance, the day I try to salve my soul. A day when I look into the burning box of memories and try to piece together a peace.

I thought that this year, maybe every year now, I'd have to find a different way to mourn and to celebrate the loss and the life of my mother, another way to measure the passing of mine. This annual reflection on her birthday has come to mean a lot to me—I feared it yet another thing lost.

But then the strongest most determined lady I ever knew passed away and something changed. I think my Nan gave me today; she reminded me of the resolve forged in our bones, the need for a steel that matches the softness of the heart. She gave me the proverbial kick I needed to lift my head and tell myself to be better than this. My ghosts, if not I, are worth more.

Today on a day when I deserve to hurt, metaphor hung heavy about me. The misted shroud the valleys cloaked themselves in, the sunshine trying to break through, the route ahead of me once easy yet now looking impossible.

Leaving the car was a climb into the unknown in many differing ways but one that today I knew I needed to try and make. As I made slow progress there were glimpses and flashes—of views and pains, of sadness and happiness. My feet followed a path I've never taken but one I know well, upwards into the cloud, towards the rock, pushing, striving, moving slowly, surely, cautiously—but moving. If not with grace, then at least with gratitude.

I've said before that I never feel truly alone in the mountains—history, hopes, ghosts and chances all walk with me, tugging on that invisible rope, guiding me, pulling me, steadying me, making me stop, take the time to stare, a weight to gladly carry onward.

Somewhere around the flanks of a raven-roosted crag the swirling of the clouds and my mind seemed to clear, I broke through the inversion. Before me a rock-strewn summit, tiny iridescent tarns reflecting azure, skylarks singing above me like angels.

Somehow I'm back in the wonder.

The finest of all cathedrals to give my thanks in.

We sat a goodly while, me, myself and my ghosts.

Both the women who shaped me from my earliest age are gone from this earthly realm now, yet today they both walked with me a ways, lifted me up, lent me their strength. I've romanticised my grandfather's memory to a level I know simply couldn't be lived up to, but the truth is my life hasn't been one of male role models. In the searching of sepia memories, faded speckled and torn, one thing holds true: both these women, women who deeply disliked each other, put that aside because both of them loved me and did the very best they could for me. Wise women would once say there is power in the naming of things; and these women, a mother and a grandmother, named me, though decades apart. I still carry my given name, but when I chose to change my family name it was a play on words that felt true, my family name becoming the name my nan would call me when we were alone, a name that wrapped a little boy in love. When I told my mum what my new chosen name was she smiled a wry smile and said "you've chosen well".

It took me a long time to see that my mum, cowed, scared and lost still did what she could to protect me, though that often that meant sending me away, or things a little boy and an angry teenager can't grasp… and yet, when I was sent away it was to the farm. My nan's presence was everywhere, strong, loyal, and formidable: a true farming woman, the beating heart of the land. I think she sowed in me values and attributes I've only realised the benefit of in the dark of this latter life.

This has become the day when I introspect, when I pause and ponder, when I wander into the wonder to give thanks and to ask of myself questions I know I'll never find all the answers for.

But today amidst the sorrow and the pain there was happiness, gratitude and love.

Today I answered some questions about myself and gave a lot of thanks.

Today I held the darkness at bay and walked in the light.

Today I remembered and today I smiled.

April 9th 2019 Giving Thanks; reasons to smile.

I'm lucky that I get to walk and wander in this my cathedral often, but there is one day of the year I now come to simply be. To be paused but present, connected again to the world all around.

It's not a cathedral where I come for an absolution I'll never receive, or to repent mistakes I can't unmake. It's certainly not a place where I'd take any sermon with grace. But it is here, more often than any other place, that I find my path forward, it's here I come closest to understanding so much.

Nine years.

Nine years since she was killed.

Gone. Taken. Not lost.

I'd struggle to find a way to describe how long these nine last years have been, how much my world has changed or the ways in which I've tried to rebuild both myself and the life I'm lucky enough to live. Trying not to fall back into the abyss, trying to honour her by being more, something better, or even just by still being here.

And yet… in so many ways there are, and always will be, times when it feels like not a moment has passed—when the weight of her murder holds me fast to a past that has too much gravity to ever escape, when the dark depths had hold, when that was all I believed I deserved. There are still many days when I think that it should be the everything of my existence, for what could or should ever matter more? How is aught else anything but a distraction, a fool's illusion cast to hide away an awful shaded truth?

But, thankfully, and with grace, but….

Those moments are few and though they are hard to endure I'm beginning to know how to survive them. Nine years has for the most part let me recognise the darkening of the day, master the moments of lost and they now seldom take me by surprise, rarely do they own all of me anymore. Now I choose to look for the stars shining brightly that the dark no longer dims, I focus on their light, I try to celebrate rather than mourn.

The memory of a smile, the lost music of a laugh, the remembered touch of a hand on my face—they all now carry more meaning than the remorse of regret or the desire for retribution. All help me understand that moving on is the only right way to celebrate who my mother was and the love she gave us all, the only way to be the son she wanted to raise.

Whilst it's true I'll never hold Mum again, that I'll miss her every day, I've come to know she's not gone from this world. Because there's love in the world if we look for it, there's love in the world if we choose to give it forth. I know more than most that there is good and evil in here too—but I also now know that there's far more good, more truth, more love. That's the legacy we leave behind, that's how we stay in the world.

Today on my mother's birthday we sat together under a glorious sky and watched a little puppy play on her first Wainwright. We talked of the hard years gone and the better years ahead, we remembered other loved ones now passed and gave thanks for those still here.

We looked out into the world and we smiled, and that was enough. More than enough.

Whilst Blipfoto and the journaling ostensibly seem like just a recording of events there was a lot more going on, lots that I didn't even recognise or appreciate at the time. Slowly I started to interact, to communicate, to give and receive. Almost uniquely, in my personal experience of social media, the site was and remains an oasis of supportive positivity. A decade later I watch incredulously as Facebook groups set up to support those with mental health issues become angry echo chambers amplifying negativity; on Blip if people don't agree with a view you express they simply don't comment that day and are nearly always a lot of loveliness the next. The simple act of purposely setting out to find something to photograph and record as a record of each day, multiplied by the sharing of it openly and honestly with strangers, has been immensely cathartic. Some Blippers, as they're known, have become 'real-world' friends, some real-world friends have become Blippers, but the vast majority of the wonderful people who've encouraged and supported me are people I'll never meet spread across the globe. And that was quite a turning point for me conceptually, I suspect it probably is for a lot of folk. To experience then prove and finally believe that the default setting for strangers was good rather than the media-driven concept of bad—that wasn't something I was expecting. It made me lift my head up and look, really look, out into the world. It still does. Every single day.

But there were other subtle and not so subtle changes that slowly helped me start to remember what it was to smile again.

Out on the trail in the Alps I could feel tension disappear. Walking longer routes such as the Tour du Mont Blanc or from Chamonix to Zermatt and back with weather excellent, excellently bad and seldom in between felt somehow meaningful, the manifestation of a me that I could want to be, a version of me that people could like again. Often lost to my own internal reverie I couldn't tell you when I started to notice how everyone, and I mean everyone, greeted their fellow trekkers on the trail with a cheery "Bonjour"—even as I wandered a circular route through three countries it stayed a constant. For so long I'd scowled at strangers, avoided them, felt triggered and ready to strike first. I really didn't want to be somebody you'd choose to talk to. But as the tension dropped from my shoulders, slowly, subconsciously, I began to say it myself. I think it took me by surprise but I found I liked it, often not even a break in our strides, but a greeting, a positive acknowledgement, the occasional nod towards a magnificent view. And then of course you'd meet other English—speaking travellers and they'd want to chat. Often they'd see my guide's badge and have questions and I'd discover it felt good to help, to give a little of something that cost me naught. At first the superficial nature of these conversations fixed me fast in the now, these people didn't know me, couldn't—in my mind—judge me, in fact saw me as a positive. They forced me from the past into the present. More time travelling.

It's hard not to smile when you're surrounded by majesty, its genuinely difficult to say bonjour in a non-cheery way, and these transient moments with strangers all slowly helped knock some of the sharper edges off me. And even more slowly it became a thing. Back in the UK I'd make a point of being that person who greeted you with a smile and hello (ok, ok, I did continue saying bonjour for a while) and now, many years later I'm always the guide that stops and asks how you are, the person who offers to take your photo, I now make an effort to be one of the nicest people you meet in your day. And I'm doing it unconsciously, it's become a part of who I am, chosen change made real. I didn't know it back then but one simple word was all it took to begin to cast a spell.

There were other physical indications of that slow metamorphosis, simple things that I did to differentiate past and present, things that put a smile on my and other people's faces, became a part of a newer happier me. It wasn't just the grin or the cheery greeting you'd notice—I'm usually the guide you'll see from a distance away. For a long time after Mum I always wore black, and not just in mourning. I had so many sombre things to do—court, lawyers, talks… they all had a social expectation. But even before then it had been my colour of choice for years. And it wasn't just me. Ask any guide who works outside of the UK and they'll all tell you they can always identify the Brits—they're the ones wearing boring black, dull grey or dismal dark blue. As I walked and stopped and spoke to people out in the bright sun I also noticed how vibrant the French or Italian Guides looked, some in uniforms of electric blue and orange, others wearing green or pink. As I settled into a guide's life in France I could see the benefit; easy to recognise, easy to follow. I bought a pair of bright green trousers, bright blue and orange shirts and set out with clients. Every one of them commented. It was a comfort to know where I was, to know help was close by if they needed it, to know who the leader was. All positive reinforcement loops shoring up my self's sense of purpose. I like this visual representation of a transformed me, a different me, a me of now not then. Nowadays I'll not just guide in bright clothes; they're my everyday choice.

The transitory unknowable nature of clients and new climbing partners made out on the trails and crags was a real boon it took me a while to understand the magic of. Being paid to make peoples' dream holiday a reality, investing yourself in making their time with you special, working hard to achieve a personal goal—all were a spiritual meditation in appreciating the moments when seen through others' eyes, mastering empathy, in the giving of yourself for others benefit. To see those others often struggle with what I'd find easy, both physically and mentally, was both humbling and empowering. Each trip I'd learn to observe and assess people better, who needed a gentle word, who sought silence, where to alter the way, when to say enough. I started to make more connections with people at an emotional level and—this was the key for me —at *their* emotional level. For the first time in years something else, someone else, usually several someones, occupied my days. The necessity, the rightness, of putting clients first put my darker thoughts away for a while, fixed me fast in time and space for the first time in too long. I became mindful not just of myself but of others again.

It was (and remains) both physically and mentally hard work. Being occupied mind and body from opening to closing your eyes, often for days at a time, gave me the most amazing relief from the voices in the dark, made me sleep, helped me heal. Dealing with the variables of weather, terrain and—the most challenging of all—people left me both shattered and invigorated. I'd not fully realised just how bad my nights had become. Little or no sleep had become normalised, its restorative powers for the mind as well as the body forgotten. To finish my days and fall deep to sleep was a kind of magic I'd lost any understanding of.

Unlike when I'd first run away to the Alps this latter life me wasn't trying to distract a screaming mind, wasn't seeking to push close to consequence in the hope of a momentary emptiness; this me was simply busy doing a good thing with nearly always good people. Another of those questions that crop up with regular frequency is "how come you're happy to do the same treks again and again?" and the very simplified answer is that it's the people that make each of these trips unique and special—everyone has a story to tell, everyone will bring something to the endeavour. They'll have moments of doubt, moments where they struggle and in helping them in those very moments I'll be more than I was, I'll feel a sense of purpose and reward.

And even then that's the dumbed down version of it all. Because simply by being here (and by here I mean in the mountains, wherever those mountains may be) I'm returning to the place where that first spark of happiness took hold again when I was wandering lost in the dark. I'm returning to the memory palace where I find it easiest to see myself at peace. In immersing myself in the place I now know I'm happiest, and creating a self-fuelled self-fulfilling prophecy.

But there's another truth to mountaineering. The friendships you do make—even the ones that don't last the test of linear time—they're deep, solid friendships. There are very few climbers or mountaineers that will push themselves without a partner they trust. As I began to tie on with old friends, new friends, strangers met for the day I knew, knew in the climber's core of myself that I had to be bombproof again. I had to be dependable, I had to do the right thing. After five years solely focused on the things I'd not done, on a me I never thought I'd be, forcing myself to step up, to put people's lives in my hands, it helped me see a different me—the me, perhaps that these people saw, the me, perhaps I could be, should be, again. Just possibly the me my mum saw.

It's hard to spend long hours on a route or days on the trail and not get to know each other well. Standing on a summit, abseiling off a cliff into the unknown or simply staring into the embers of a fire with a drink in your hand are all undertakings almost perfectly crafted to elicit moments of deep connection and honesty. Swapping details of who we'd call if it all went wrong, making quick abiding decisions with other peoples' lives—it all brought into clear focus the importance of that which remained to be lost, and did the same for the behaviours of my own recent past. As business friends disappeared at a rate that almost exactly matched my usefulness to them, so I began to make new friends, friends that only knew this latter version of me, hadn't seen that darker, lost me. And one by one as those friendships blossomed—some over hours, some over months—I started to tell people my tragic family history. It felt right that they should know all of me, even if I didn't want that history to be the only all of me anymore. I was met with the most amazing amount of support and love. Nobody reacted in the way I expected or feared. People who engage with the outdoors are, in my experience, almost always more empathetic and accepting, I think it's part of the process. Alert to the moments; moments of risk, success, failure, moments of happiness, relief or simple survival, it makes you alert to so much more. These are people who choose to test themselves, who work and play in a theatre rich with consequence. Whilst few will thankfully ever be forged in the sort of fires that I had been, many had experienced sudden loss, knew this fleeting thing we call life is to be celebrated, had found their own paths to a better tomorrow.

There's no respite or joy to be taken or found in another's sorrows or suffering—and I hesitate to use the word comfort—but there is a camaraderie, a common ground of understanding, to be found with others who know the meaning of the risks you've taken, who've had their own moments of realisation. As we walked and talked, when we were sat on high belays or buried in freezing snowholes, I found that so many of the people I met had also survived terrible childhoods, been bullied at school, abused at home, reinvented themselves, worked amazingly hard, sacrificed so much more than most—all to be the version of themselves that was happy.

They almost always knew what it meant to fly.

They were, it transpired, just the people I needed to be spending time with. They were, and remain, people who smile a lot.

Chapter 8

Shining Stars

In the depths of depression, the darkness can seem all—consuming, overwhelming, like it's the only thing that truly exists. You find yourself painfully prying open long-locked boxes full of old regrets, re-living the same unanswered questions over and over. When you're that far gone it feels inevitable that the worst moments from the last decade and more will shape and shade everything else. And in those awful moments, it's easy to let the pain of the past define your entire life. For a long time, that was my reality. My mother's death and the brutal way it tore through everything became the sole lens through which I viewed myself. It took from me not just my mother all but the last of the light I saw in the world.

But that shouldn't be all of who I am. It's not the whole of my story, and it isn't the only thing that has shaped the life I live today. I lost sight of that for far too long, but that truth has come to be the foundation of my recovery and, in many ways, my redemption.

There are things I should have always known, truths I feel were always with me, that seemed elusive, impossible to grasp, or even believe. Even on the darkest of nights, there are always an infinite number of stars if we can only look for them in the moments of clarity. Yet, too often, we miss them. Their light flickers and fades, and our heads stay bowed, lost in grief, depression or worse. We forget to look up. But when you finally lift your eyes and see just one star—when you truly see it with everything you are—its light can guide you back to somewhere better, brighter.

It can take a lifetime to understand that the stars are always there, whether we see them or not. They should be our focus, especially when we realise we're lost. Yes, it can feel impossible to believe in the existence of light when you're trapped by the weight of the abyss.

Yet as I look back, I've come to understand something important: my path was always lit, even when I thought I was walking in shadows. There were moments, people, lights along the way that steered me, even when I wasn't aware of them. They were there, some constant, some new and some unknown—but all shining stars lending me their light, even when I believed I was utterly alone.

The gift of this journey, of hindsighted words, is the release of being free of time. I can choose to honour those stars today, for this story isn't really about the darkness, though it held me for so long. Nor is it a tale of mountains or endeavour. Really it's about the light I found and the souls who sheltered and nurtured it, helped it to grow—all those who played a part in leading me back to a life of love.

If I allowed myself to focus only on the bad times, I could easily believe that my childhood was nothing but sorrow, that my mother's murder was the inevitable culmination of that. Depression would have me think that way, convincing me that her death overshadowed all her life. But if I chose only to see her in death, if I let the manner of her death define her, then I would lose her entirely. If I never let myself remember her warmth, her smile, her love, then she would be truly gone. The stars—those moments of love—remind me that even in loss, even in grief, love remains.

Does a beating deserve more space in my heart than a hug? Do my childhood scars matter more than the gentle whispers of my grandfather as he rocked me to sleep? When I close my eyes, which image do I want to see—that awful forensic outline, or the radiant smile that lit up the room?

Which do we value more? Today's love or yesterday's pain?

And perhaps more importantly, what if the love was there all along, waiting for me to see it? What if it wasn't the love that was missing, but my ability to believe in it? Love is an often intangible magic that works on us even when we don't see it, even when we're lost.

I've thought on this endlessly, during many long, lonely journeys into the mountains. It's a question that has lifted my eyes, urged me to examine every path I've walked, each decision I've made. It's held me still in moments of doubt, as if the very air in those high places stood waiting for me to understand something deeper, something more essential. And yet, it has also driven me forward—toward an answer, a revelation I had not expected to find. What was it that made me search for the stars rather than allow myself to slip silently into the abyss? When the hammer blow of losing Mum shattered my world, as depression and worse took hold, what was it that gave me the strength to rise again, to try and find a way to take those steps towards better?

Revisiting these thoughts, now softened by the passing of years, I find the question itself has shifted in meaning. It was never truly *what* that guided me through the shadows—it was *who*. These souls, scattered like stars across the landscape of my life,

145

were the ones who offered their light, their belief, at moments when I had none of my own.

It is easy, in the aftermath of pain, to search for a single cause, a reason for our survival, our resilience. But now, with the clarity that comes from looking back, I understand that strength is rarely solitary. So many people lent me their strength, helped me find my way out of the dark.

Love. Not a word I heard often growing up, not something that echoed in the walls of my childhood home, nor something that wove itself into the fabric of my early life, no part of my sense of self. If I close my eyes and search for it, I can only really recall it with any true warmth in my grandfather's voice—spoken softly, quietly, by someone who understood the worth of its weight. For the longest time, I couldn't have told you what it meant, not really. It was something distant, abstract, a concept that seemed to belong to other people, other lives. It wasn't until much, much later that I came to know its real shape, its depth, and its power.

Yet, as I look back on my latter years, I realise love has always been by my side, often unspoken but always present. Love that showed itself in quiet ways if only I'd been looking, revealing its reality in moments both monumental and mundane. It tethered me to the past, anchoring me to the echoes of those long gone, while at the same time, it reached forward, connecting me to the present, to people who became my lifeline when I needed it most. There's a curious contradiction in this, a paradox that took me years to unravel—because for so long, I believed that love existed in separate worlds, belonging to separate parts of myself. It was a coping mechanism I'd learned young, keeping love at a distance, boxed away where it couldn't be taken, stolen, broken. But that separation didn't serve me; it only left me lonelier, made me weaker.

Then I fell into love. And it really was a fall: sudden and breathtaking. I didn't expect it, didn't plan for it. It happened all at once, sweeping me into another current I didn't know existed. She was the most beautiful girl, and though it took me far too long to say the words, to admit even to myself that I felt it, the truth of it was undeniable. Even harder to fathom was the realisation that she felt it too. After so long spent alone— emotionally distant, fiercely independent—it was incredible to find myself part of something bigger, something shared. Love didn't just sit beside us; it enveloped us, grew with us, became something greater. As my relationship with Mum changed and fractured, as always frail familial bonds finally began to fail, my wife became my centre, my constant. Together, we were stronger, our love deepening through every shared experience.

But then, that dreadful day. Losing Mum was like being struck by a lightning, a force so powerful that it shattered everything in its path, including my belief in the power of love. And there, amidst the wreckage, both real and metaphorical, was my wife. Her strength was immense. The kind of strength that could only ever be born through love. But as the horror of events stretched out through months and years, as my grief and guilt pulled me down into the depths, I began to fear that I would pull her down with me, drag her into the same dark abyss. I'd already failed one love; what right did I have to risk another? Those thoughts haunted me, whispered cruelly that I was undeserving, that I was a burden too heavy to bear.

And yet. I never saw her waver. There she was, by my side, every day. Often unappreciated, but always there. She held me up when I was certain I would fall. She gave me the courage to keep going, to keep believing, even when I had no belief left in myself. Love was there all along. It was love that showed me the way forward.

There are times when the abyss seems all—consuming, when you lose sight of everything that matters most, including yourself. In those moments, you start to lose your faith—not just in the people who love you, but in the very idea of love itself. You begin to doubt that love can endure, that it can continue unbroken, despite everything. That's the cruellest thing about the abyss: it makes you forget that true love isn't something that falters at the face of hardship. It persists. Endures not because of the absence of suffering, but in spite of it.

The farm was a place of magic for a little boy. I'm sure my stepfather thought it was some sort of punishment, sending me away, but for me it was a sanctuary. I can still recall the excitement and relief that held me still when I knew a visit was coming. It didn't matter if I wasn't told in advance; somehow, I always knew. I couldn't arrive battered and bruised—the shift in atmosphere, the sudden absence of tension, all signalled that I had survived again. Hope stirred in those moments, carrying me through to the safety of my grandparents, reinforcing my belief in flying.

I struggle to find the words to describe their love; it was quiet, constant, unconditional. It was foreign to me, and as a child, I didn't understand its true worth. How could I? I had no basis to expect that kind of care, no frame of reference for the way they simply loved me, no matter what. Only now, as an adult, do I see it for what it was: life-saving.

They'd collect me from so many strange places—never the family home, and fear and worry would fade away. We'd talk. It sounds so simple, but for me being allowed to speak without being shouted down or dismissed was a gift beyond measure. To be listened to, to be heard, really heard, moments of my own truth, moments of right. I knew I was safe, headed somewhere I didn't have to be scared.

The farm was a world far larger in my mind than it was in reality. I'd press my face against the windows, stretching on tiptoes to glimpse the far horizon, convinced that the fields stretched to the ends of the earth. I never questioned it, and my grandfather encouraged a belief that we were lords of all we surveyed.

I wandered the farm freely, exploring barns and sheds filled with towering tractors and harvesters, playing in fields, and visiting animals. The workers welcomed me, showing me how things worked, letting me steer the machines. I can still recall the distant uncle who saved a grass snake in his pocket, waiting for me to wander by. The lady with the goat who'd bring him to our gate each evening, the horses I knew to bring apples to— each one a piece of the magic.

As my home life worsened so the farm's meaning only deepened. It wasn't just a place, it was a refuge, a beacon. If I could endure just one more day, survive a little longer, then I'd find myself back at the farm again, safe in its embrace. But the real magic wasn't in the place itself. It was in the hope and love that filled it.

Even as the farm changed—shrinking, neglected, parts sold off—it remained my sanctuary. The gardens might have fallen into disrepair, but the memories still bloomed. The love my grandparents gave me, the lessons they taught me, lingered long after the physical space had faded. And in times of trouble I'd return, find the ghost of my grandfather, hear again his gentle voice, and feel the love that never left me push away the shadows. The farm, even diminished, remained a place where I could breathe, let go of the bad, and remember what truly mattered.

Now, as I look back, I see that the boy who wandered those fields, who was so nearly lost to anger and hurt... he found his way through love. The lasting magic of the farm wasn't about size or worth, but in the strength it gave me. The strength to stand, to heal, to be whole. It taught me that better existed, and it wove an unseen thread of love into my understanding of the world.

Other distant stars taught me other lessons perhaps not as profound as the power of love, but lessons that helped shape me —helped guide me, literally saved me, became fundamental parts of who I am now. The sort of lessons everyone has through a life, lessons it's so easy to forget.

When life at home finally got unliveable I jumped into the betwixt and left. Not yet old enough to drive, conditioned to be ashamed of who I was, believing that leaving meant lost, meant loser—I just left. Knowing that going back would never be an option again. I walked out of the door with no idea of what came next.

I should have gone to the farm, I should have known to, but the truth is that in our worst moments, when fear finds a way for the darkness to take hold, then it's easy to be lost so much quicker than you could ever think possible. When you believe you're worthless it can be impossible to look for the light. Sometimes we need one of those stars to find us.

The first night I slept under the pier. I think anger probably kept me warm. Little England in February isn't life threateningly cold, but it's equally not great. For a few days I broke into sheds and cars just to sleep somewhere that felt momentarily safe. I washed in café toilets, ate at other people's house, at work. At the weekend I got drunk, lied to whomever asked about where I'd been all week and crashed on any floor I could find. Week two I discovered the boats at Lytham marina—better equipped, not used

150

in winter and easier to break into. I'd no great plan. Sometime in week three I was cadging food at my best mate's house, just happening to be there every mealtime, thinking I was hiding my situation well. Still too ashamed to tell the truth. And his dad, a small slight man, just came straight out with it and asked me if I was sleeping rough, then told me he knew I was, told me I was staying with them that night. He didn't ask for an explanation, he just knew and he stepped up.

He put his hand on my arm, gave it a gentle squeeze and said "it'll be OK".

Three decades later I'm paused by those three words that lifted my eyes, showed me another path, gave me a hope of something better. Over the next few weeks Mr Y did more than I could ever repay. He went round to my parents' house and came back with a bag that had the last of my belongings that hadn't been thrown out. He got me back into a school I can only believe would have been glad to be rid of me. He helped me through the interminable difficulties of getting a flat from Social Services in Thatcher's Britain in the mid 1980s.

I can't tell you exactly how or definitively when, but a lifetime later I can tell you why. He did it because, and the utter simplicity of this, the mind-bending complexity, it still stops me in my tracks—he did it because it was the right thing to do. We know deep down, we all know. And then we make choices. He did it because it was the right thing to do, that's what good people do. A psychodynamic counsellor might tell you right and wrong are constructs we develop in our super-ego, early, hidden, deep inside. I'm not saying they're wrong. Your priest would offer a different ideological viewpoint. I'm not saying they'd be wrong either. I've spent a long time on a metaphysical couch and I don't believe in that God anymore; yet I do believe we all have a soul. I think that's where right and wrong live.

Did I learn that lesson then? Was that the moment I learned that there are far more good people in the world than bad? The reality of being the writer sat here both then and now is I know I don't know. The wonder of time travel is I can choose to believe that maybe I did. I learned it then and in so many other moments. I learned it in the light and it guided me in the dark. I just lost sight of it for too long a time.

I know I'll have said thanks, I'll have meant it with all my little heart. But when you're so close to the rocks you're usually too busy trying not to drown to really think about the people who man the lighthouse. I know I've carried that gratitude always; sometimes I'll detour to drive past the house where Mr Y lived in the way I imagine a Catholic might light a candle, or a Buddhist add a flag. But it took the crucible of Mum to really pause and look, to join the dots, to realise how Mr Y, and others too long unacknowledged, helped light my passage through the decades, gave me the strength to be here today.

The love of good grandparents is a blessing, one that most people can understand and appreciate. But Mr. Y stands tall in my mind, in my personal inner world. I've known for as long as I can remember that I owe him a debt I could never repay. But in trying to trace the path from then to now, I started to see that so many other, long forgotten, seldom acknowledged stars had also guided me, their light unseen in my immediate memory but a part of my much greater whole.

When I left home that night, I was working at the local fish and chip shop. I kept showing up for my shifts, even though the shop was almost within sight of my stepfather's house. I kept turning up, I kept being paid, and I kept getting fed—I'd forgotten that part. At the time, I'm sure I just took it for granted, but it wasn't normal. I've run takeaways later in life, and they don't feed their staff every night. They don't give them a clean top each day when it's clear they've worn the same clothes for a week.

It's not just the big moments that change a life.

When I think back on the experiences I now see as transformative, I realise how many of them were made up of small moments, little gestures of kindness that went unnoticed at the time. There were the Scout leaders who took us away from abusive home lives without a word, who didn't bother about subs, or uniforms, or badges, but simply offered us a place of respite. There were the parents of schoolfriends who let me sleep on their couches, fed me so I didn't have to go home. Even the local landlady who gave me a job and a place to be in the pub, years earlier than she should have—so long as I behaved.

But when I remembered, relearned, and began to believe again in the truth of these next words, I knew I had a chance—more than a chance—of finding my way back to a life I loved again:

There are so many more heroes than we ever know.

Those little bits of help as you stumble, the steady arm when you falter, the small good deeds done simply because they're the right thing to do... they are the very real, gentle magic in the world.

It's early 2010. I'm that Kelvyn, the one you don't want to meet. I've walked into town with the banking run for the business. Almost hunched with an ever-present internal rage I've carried every day since she was killed. Looking back I genuinely think I've started taking the cash up to the bank—a menial job I've not done in years— just in the hope someone will try and take it off me, just to have a reason to hurt someone, to let some part of the dark out.

It's 2010. I'm still lost, still believe in the old answers. And I'd guess I look it, dressed in black, a lot heavier, menace in every movement. My mind has drifted again, I'm just stood by the bandstand in the middle of town when I'm broken from thoughts that won't have been anywhere near pleasant by a soft gentle voice next to me. I look down and there she is: a little old lady with a grandmother's headscarf and handbag. She puts a hand on my arm and I flinch inside.

"You're that young man aren't you? The one whose mother was killed?"

The way I draw in my next breath is the only affirmation I give, so often in my life that would have been a warning you'd do well to heed. I'm paused, betwixt... and then she hugs me, really hugs me and says "God bless you, always remember your mum loved you very much"

I don't know how long it took me to become aware of where I was again. I remember being on a bench by the river, probably half a mile away from our encounter, eyes puffy with tears. It's been a long time since I've believed in the kind of God she spoke of, but I can tell you that I've come to believe in people a lot. It's a belief I'd forgotten for so long, it's a belief that I saw the spark of again that day with an unknown little old lady. I can appreciate that maybe it was her own God who gave her the strength to do that, but when I look back I don't see a mystical divinity, I see the physically divine: the real magic of human kindness.

I've thought of her often, though I don't remember her face. I don't know if I spoke to her or what I might have said. But I do remember how she both broke and saved me that day. A kind stranger gave me something I hadn't realised I needed: a touchstone, a human connection to something more than my inner world, something to reach for as I fell. When everything seemed unimaginably lost, when I was willingly walking into the dark, she reminded me that there's love in the world—not just the personal love we know from those closest to us, but the inherent love built into life itself. That goodness exists, even when we can't see it.

Assumptions about then versus now. I'm not the me I was anymore, how can you love the me I am now?

Unconditional positive regard. Three small words, yet vast in their significance. If you're familiar with them, then I applaud you—whether you've been on the receiving end of such a gift, or whether you've had the strength and compassion to offer it to another, I say well done. For those words carry a magic beyond measure, a quiet, unassuming power that can shift the course of a life, or perhaps, as I've come to understand, simply save it.

There is a point in this telling where I'll speak about the profound change that comes from talking, really talking, with others. But perhaps, by then, I will have also come to understand something even simpler, something quietly transformative: that it's not just the talking that heals, but what comes before. It's the simple gift of companionship, the presence of another soul that begins to dissolve the walls of solitude. Sometimes it's the person who sits with you in the dark, the one who wanders in the wonder at your side, simply is. The time spent not alone, the gentle exchange of understanding and the sharing of moments, that somehow shifts the focus, makes talking possible when words seem too far out of reach.

We often underestimate the power of these small, human connections. How a shared silence can speak louder than the longest conversation. How a moment of unspoken understanding can crack open the hardest shell. It's not always the grand gestures or the deep revelations that matter, but the quiet offering of time, attention, and presence. The warmth of being accepted, not for what you should be, but for who you are in that moment, flaws, fears, and all. It is in these moments, simple as they seem, that we start to connect again. We see we are not as lost, as broken, or as unreachable as we thought.

And so, those three words symbolise a kind of magic. The simple kindness of assuming the best of us or others, the soft reassurance that they are worthy just as we are. In that space, even the most hesitant among us might find the strength to speak, and in speaking, to begin again.

So many people lit candles for me during the darkest of times—most without even knowing it. Their kindness, their presence, was often instinctive, a reflection of who they were. To try and list them all would be impossible, not because they're forgotten, but because the light they brought was immeasurable, woven into the very fabric of my recovery.

These are the words I've wrestled with the most, though I once thought they'd spill easily onto the page. How do you thank the countless souls who likely have no idea of the weight they lifted from your shoulders? How do you express the worth of what they did, when their faces are now blurred by time and memory?

I can only offer my gratitude in the form of an amalgamation— a climbing partner here, a trail companion there, an occasional kind stranger in between—all gathered together in my heart, one sweeping, silent *thank you*. I hope, somehow, it's enough. Enough to let them know who they were, who they are, and who they'll always be to me: the ones who lit the way when I couldn't see it myself, the ones who, by simply being there, gave me hope.

I find myself in a car with three strangers, our friendships not yet forged, but a shared purpose has bound us together. We're enroute to an International Mountain Leader training course in the French Alps. The journey is long, and the conversation is polite but cautious—each of us feeling the unspoken weight of what lies ahead. When we finally arrive at the auberge, we're the last to join the group. It's 2013, and though I still don't quite see myself as a

156

'group person', I'm clinging to anything mountain-related to silence the voices I hear in the dark. Being here means more than I can easily put into words.

Room assignments are simple, based only on gender and age. Nothing more. My roommate is Spike. We exchange a nod, neither of us entirely sure what to expect. As we unpack, the room fills with a quiet awkwardness. Both of us, as it turns out, have brought a bottle of Scotch—perhaps hoping it might break the ice or ease the tension, but maybe to help us sleep. We exchange glasses, and just as I take a deep breath to say, "There's something I think you should know... I might talk, shout, or scream in the night..." Spike speaks at the same time, and the exact same words spill from his mouth.

It takes a moment for the coincidence to sink in, but we both laugh, the tension easing. Over the next few hours, we shared our stories—each of our horrors deeply personal, perhaps unimaginable to the other, and yet somehow easy to understand. So many coincidences—events out of our control shaping us, making us question who we thought we were. The filth of our gutter press, the weight of social expectation the voices of those who knew none of the detail. There was an instant empathy, a knowing. Not because our experiences were the same, but because the emotional scars they left had a similar weight. Strangers, yet connected by the way our separate paths had shaped us, by the way tragic events still threatened to define us.

We stayed up late into the night, and then well into the early hours, slowly letting out some of the burdens we carried. In sharing, we found solace. We acknowledged the difficult and life-changing experiences we'd had, recognising that, in different ways, we had both spent time lost in the dark, were both looking for a way to find our true selves again. Chance had placed us together, yet that night reminded me we are never truly alone. The abyss may feel personal, but it calls to far more of us than we realise. A decade has passed since then, and I rarely see Spike. Yet when we do meet, there is an unspoken bond, a trust, a deep understanding. It is the kind of love I was slow to comprehend, the kind I've learned to recognise in the mountains and on the trail—a love born not of romance, but of shared experience, from empathy and understanding, of trust forged in extremis.

And it wasn't just Spike. Many people like him have kept me grounded, laughing with me, trusting me to venture into the unknown alongside them. They've chose to believe in my strength when I struggled to think I had any. So many of them had been lost before they found their way to the mountains, just as I had.

Years after that first trip to the Alps, I found myself in the Scottish Highlands, guiding a small group through the rugged beauty of Glen Coe. We were an odd mix of people, as these trips often gathered—a few seasoned adventurers, a couple of first-timers, and one man, J, who stood alone, unsure.

J wasn't like the others. While the rest of the group chatted easily, laughing and sharing stories as we trekked through mist-covered valleys, he remained mostly silent, keeping to the back. There was something in his eyes that reminded me of Spike and many others I'd met by then, something in his silence that spoke volumes. It was a familiar sight—the look of someone who had faced their own shadows, who had spent long hours in the dark lands and was still finding their way out. I didn't push him to talk, I knew from experience that the mountains have a way of loosening the most tightly held burdens. So I waited.

It wasn't until the third day that J began to open up. We had just reached the summit of Buachaille Etive Mòr, the wind biting at our faces, the valley spread out like a painting below us. The rest of the group had scattered slightly, taking in the view, when J came to stand next to me. For a moment, we just stood there, the silence between us comfortable, heavy with unspoken thoughts. Then, without prompting, he began to speak.

He told me of a loss that had almost broken him, of how he had spent years in a haze of grief, isolating himself from the world, from everyone he loved. The mountains had been his refuge, the one place where the weight of it all didn't feel quite so suffocating. But he had always walked alone, never joining a group, never trusting himself to be something other than his own sorrow. Until now.

I listened quietly as he spoke, understanding all too well what he was describing. It was the same story I had heard from so many before him, my own story, a story repeated by so many of those who came to the wilderness seeking something, even if they didn't know exactly what. J wasn't looking for answers. He was looking for connection, for a way back into the world. And the mountains, with their vastness and their silence, had somehow shown him a path forward.

When he finished speaking, we stood there a while longer, the wind tugging at our jackets, and then we made our way down to join the others. J walked at my side for the rest of the day, his pace matching mine, and something had shifted in him. He still didn't say much, but the tension in his shoulders had eased, the weight he carried just a little lighter.

In the days that followed, I watched as J slowly became part of the group. He was still quiet, still reserved, but there was a kindness in his actions, the occasional smile on his face. He would stop from time to time and look all around, as if with fresh eyes, somehow he looked like this was where he was truly meant to be.

It struck me then, as it has many times since, that people who find their way into nature, especially those who choose to do it with others, are often the ones who have been through their own dark times, who are the most empathetic, the most aware of the unspoken struggles that others carry. Nature has a way of stripping us down to our essentials, of revealing who we really are, and it attracts those who are willing to be vulnerable in that space.

In the wilderness, there are no distractions, no screens to hide behind. When you're out there with someone, you see them for who they truly are. And in that raw, open space, there is room for a kind of connection that those who have walked through their own darkness understand. They know what it feels like to be lost, to struggle, and they offer compassion freely, without judgement. These are the people who taught me that empathy is not just a reaction to suffering—it's a form of strength, a type of love that comes from an understanding of our shared humanity.

The mountains, the trails, they attract those who have been broken, but who have found a way to piece themselves back together. It's why I keep returning, why I choose to walk these paths with others. There is something powerful in the way we engage with each other out here, something healing in the act of being seen and understood, even in silence.

A hundred feet below, just out of sight, D waits patiently, listening for the call he's been longing to hear: "climb when ready." I know this route has been in his mind for half a lifetime—twice before he's backed away from it unconfident, choosing to hope for it on a better day. Now, from my perch high above, the world unfolds beneath me, Chamonix spread out like a distant map, its tiny white specks reminding me how far we've come physically and metaphorically. I feel the tension in my core as I sit back into the belay and lean out over the drop, my body responding instinctively to the exposure. But there's a quiet certainty within me too. *I've got this.* We're not just climbing a mountain; we're creating memories that will burn bright, even in the dimmest of days.

As I take in the rope, each gentle coil brings D closer, not just physically, but in trust, in bond. Soon, his life will be held in my hands—and not just his life, but a piece of something more profound. His sense of self, his dreams, his deepest aspirations are tied to this climb, and in these precious moments, they are entrusted to me. With each pull of the rope, that responsibility becomes tangible, an invisible thread of trust stretching between us, binding us more deeply than words ever could.

The rope comes tight. "Climb when ready," I call, and I know the words echo through him with the weight of years of anticipation. He begins to move, and we're linked not just by that rope but by something less visible yet far more powerful, faith in one another.

The final stretch of the route eases into a light-hearted traverse over a series of gendarmes, playful and almost casual after the intensity of the climb. We step into the lift station, the tourists oblivious to what has just passed between us. They snap photos, unaware of the quiet triumph in our hearts. We pack away axes and crampons, the weight of the mountain replaced by something lighter, but far more enduring.

D turns to me, and for a long moment, he holds me in a quiet, solid embrace. There's no need for words. It's the kind of love that comes from shared challenge, the kind of bond only forged in the crucible of trust and effort. Then, we laugh—because sometimes the deepest connections are felt in silence, and sometimes they rise to the surface in joy. This is the quiet, unspoken love of camaraderie, formed in so many moments like these, where challenge, trust, and friendship blend into something that lasts long after the climb is over.

And I know there are loves that fade, relationships that stumble, and moments where bitterness lingers like a shadow.

People will hurt you, make selfish choices, and sometimes leave you standing alone, wondering where it all went wrong. That's just life. It's messy, unpredictable, and often unfair. But here's the thing—despite the heartache, despite the mistakes and missteps, the love that existed doesn't just vanish. It leaves a mark. Even if the connection seems to have withered away, the love that was once shared, no matter how brief, still radiates. It lingers in the quiet corners of memory, in the lessons it leaves behind.

Yes, people will fail you. They'll say the wrong things, act out of fear or anger, and sometimes they'll do things you can't quite forgive. But we're all human, stumbling through this life, trying to make sense of it as we go. And though there are those rare moments when someone's actions seem monstrous, the vast majority of people—beneath their flaws and imperfections—are trying. They want to be good. They want to love, to connect, to leave the world a little brighter than they found it.

If we choose to see that in others, if we look beyond the mistakes and misunderstandings, we'll find that most people are doing their best. And maybe that's what love really is: seeing the best in others, even when they can't see it in themselves. If we all chose to seek that love, that light, the world would be a softer place.

And then, for me, there's the friends who arrived after it all. The ones who simply believed in a best me, not the worst me I'd come to expect from myself. Friends who didn't judge me on who I had been or the things I hadn't done, but rather on who I was becoming. They looked at what I did, not what I'd done. Their belief in me helped me see that perhaps I was better than I thought, that I was someone worth knowing, worth loving.

They saw a version of me that was unburdened by the weight of my past. It was something so simple but transformative: to be seen for the good you bring into the world, rather than the mistakes you've made along the way. They helped me see that the person I was working toward becoming was already there, waiting to be acknowledged.

Seeing people arrive with doubt etched on their faces and leave with elation in their steps, watching them glance at me as if I were more than I ever thought I could be… they have a belief in me I've not yet found. Before I began guiding others I had mostly ventured into the mountains alone, that had become my unhealthy norm. But now, with people relying on me, I found a different kind of growth, saw a different me I needed to be. The groups I led were often a sea of seemingly familiar faces, similar in age and status, mostly middle-aged professionals and retirees with the kind of disposable income that allowed them to walk these expensive treks. They weren't the sort of people I would have naturally found myself among. But. They all shared something deeper. A love for the wilderness, a choice to test their limits, a willingness to wander in the vast unknown. There was an unspoken bond between us. Sure, some might vote Tory, and others might hold views that made me wince. But they were my responsibility and that bond was enough for me to look beyond the differences, to be a better, less judgemental me.

It's impossible to pick out just one—except that it isn't.

A came to spend two weeks circling the highest peak in Europe, following trails perched high above steep drops. She had always been a lover of mountains, but now a pernicious fear stood in the way—postpartum vertigo had taken the joy of the wild from her and left her wondering if she belonged here anymore. But. I know a thing or two about fear. We walked, we laughed, and with time, the fear loosened its grip. There were still moments, and at first, I was there—the encouraging guide, the outreached hand at the difficult step—but slowly I knew to step back and then it was her, all her. What I realised I was seeing was something I deeply admired: bravery, a word so often thrown my way by the unknowing, a word that so often seemed to mock me from down in the abyss. Because true bravery isn't about being fearless—it's certainly isn't when I'm at play in the high mountains or lying to myself on a rockface. True bravery involves honesty and integrity, in the knowing you might not and going anyway, in the knowing you will not and going anyway, versions of me I felt I'd lost. At its simplest bravery lies in the trying of the unknown. It's about walking forward when the outcome is uncertain.

And here's where the real wonder lay—not in any of my obvious actions, but in the look on her face when she realised she could do it. That moment when she saw for herself that which I had seen all along. These moments, this connection between people, it's where something more profound takes root. It's not about me, or her, alone. It's about that shared experience, that bond that lifts us beyond what we are on our own, the bond the great outdoors facilitates like no other place I know.

Friendships grow not just from time together, but from this shared joy—a joy in the adventure itself, in seeing others become more. In these wild places, we don't just find our place in the world, we find it with each other.

Coming to believe in the goodness of people, in the idea that the world is filled with love, wasn't for me something that happened overnight. It was a slow, often painstaking process— a kind of unlearning of the fear, guilt, and self-loathing that had dominated my mind for so long. The love around me felt underserved, the love I had known felt distant, belonging to people I had lost, and in the depths of my pain, I had come to believe that I wasn't worth loving at all.

But then, in the mountains, through meeting good people like A and the community I refound on the end of a rope, I began to see glimpses of something different. It wasn't just about one person, or one moment—it was a growing realisation that the world was, in fact, filled with people who carried love within them. People who were kind, people who believed in one another, even believed in me, and people who, even without knowing it, put love out into the world just by being themselves.

With A, it was her belief in me that started to shift my perception. She trusted me unconditionally, placed her life in my hands literally, and saw the best in me, even when I couldn't. She didn't know the weight of my past, but she didn't need to. Her kindness and faith were enough to crack open the shell I had built around myself. I started to believe, even if only a little at first, that maybe the world wasn't as cruel and unforgiving as I had once thought.

And because of A I began to notice it in others around me—strangers, peers, fellow adventurers—who all carried with them a quiet and steady goodness. There were no miraculous moments that suddenly turned everything around. It was the magic of little things: a smile, a kind word, the way people supported one another on the trail, how they looked out for each other. These seemingly small acts, repeated over time, began to erode the belief that the world was a dark and loveless place.

What I began to realise was that the love I had lost—the love of my mother, my grandparents—didn't exist in isolation. It wasn't just confined to the people I had known or the past I had lived. Love, I discovered, surrounded me. Much like Newton's flow and Einstein's totality it exists unseen but ever-present if we're aware. It existed in the people I met along the way, people who had no reason to offer me anything but still did. There's something profoundly healing about seeing kindness in unexpected places.

There were my Amazing Alaskans—a bonded trekking group I met through chance who simply, immediately, made me one of their own, trusted me to guide them, advise them, saw the better me that A did rather than anything else I might have believed I was. And, just like with A, I soon discovered that some of them had also visited the abyss, had fears, worries and more. But in the mountains, the trust encouraged, required, reinforced... it made all those negatives less, invisible weight was shared, collectively we all became more. It wasn't about overcoming adversity, it was about building belief. I never carried anyone up steep alpine ladders, just my presence and encouragement got them to the top, their belief in me carried me a little of the way to better. To this day pictures of them and A hang on the wall above my desk. They make me smile every day.

The more time I spent with others, understanding the version of me they saw, finding out the versions of them they felt they were, all of us helping each other be somehow better, slowly I started to see that maybe the mistakes I thought I had made didn't define me.

It's strange how we often need to see love in the world before we can find it in ourselves. I had spent so long convinced that I wasn't worth loving, that I had failed in the most unforgivable ways, that I had closed myself off to the possibility of loving life again. But the goodness I encountered in so many people, in most people, it became a mirror reflecting back to me a truth I had forgotten: that love isn't something you earn or deserve based on perfection or past choices. It's something that exists in the world, and by being part of that world, you are inherently worthy of it.

Slowly, as I came to believe that the world was filled with love, I also started to believe that I was deserving of it. I began to understand that I didn't need to carry the guilt of my mother's death like a badge of shame. I didn't need to define myself by the pain of the past. The love I found in others allowed me to start releasing that weight, to let go of the belief that I had somehow failed in a way that made me unworthy of happiness.

And in doing so, I started to love life again. It wasn't just about surviving anymore it was about living, about finding joy in the small moments, about allowing myself to again be part of the world. The more I saw goodness in others, the more I wanted to engage, to be a part of it, to open myself up to the possibility of connection, of adventure, of love. I stopped looking for ways to hurt myself and started looking for ways to give of myself.

This shift, this opening of my heart to the world again, wasn't about erasing the past or pretending that the pain wasn't there. It was about seeing that whilst it was a part of my story, it wasn't the whole of who others saw me to be. The love I found in the world, in people like Spike and J and D and A and countless others, helped me to see that life could still be beautiful, still worth living. That the story continued.

How often do you tell your friends you love them? Really tell them, I mean: look them in the eye, wrap your arms around them, and let them know, without hesitation, without reservation, that you love them? How often do you let the weight of that word hang in the air, let its meaning be truly understood? I promise you, it's not often enough.

We move through life so quickly, skimming the surface of our relationships, caught in the currents of daily tasks, plans, and distractions. But in the mountains, something shifts. There, stripped of everything but the essentials, we find that love reveals itself in the quiet gestures, in the shared silences, in the way we support each other through the hard moments and celebrate the good ones. In those spaces, high above the world, disconnected from so much trivial, connected to so much that matters, you realise how vital it is to say the words, to express what lies just beneath the surface.

So, tell your friends you love them. Not just in passing, not just when the moment feels easy, but in the way that matters — fully, with intention. Because those words, when given with your whole heart, are the first steps towards feeling better about yourself.

Chapter 9

Wandering in Wonder

In searching for an understanding of events for so long I slowly came to realise that my own self-awareness was no longer as strong as I thought it might have been. If I didn't really know myself or my own truth anymore then how could I hope to ever understand anything else?

When I first headed back into the mountains it was essentially escapism, a way to be absent from one life, sometimes just to be gone for a while, sometimes to burn another possibility into existence for a fleetingly brief moment. All too often, I came to realise, I was hiding from the world, quite possibly hiding from myself. And therein lay the problem, even if I couldn't see it at the time. Whilst I was finding that temporary respite, I wasn't really making progress, I was just distracting myself, avoiding looking into the abyss rather than finding ways to take ownership and control of it. Having targets—something climbing and mountaineering are so good at—helped move my real world focus from then to tomorrow, and to be honest training for those tomorrows seemed beneficial to some of my recovery. But largely it was an endeavour in distraction, the obfuscation of creating a purpose almost always inevitably leading to lows that were just as pronounced as the peaks I climbed and just as difficult to overcome. As I became fitter and more competent in the mountains it took even more for me to be able to reach the empty space inside that was the only refuge I'd found.

But an empty thing is seldom a thing we value or love. Increasingly I needed to go further, higher, closer to the edge— and as the risks got bigger their effectiveness became less and less. I knew that I was my happiest me in the mountains, I knew that there were moments when I felt so close to an understanding of so much, but I was also coming to realise that risk and exhaustion weren't doing me the sort of good I really needed or, worse—they might be beginning to cause me harm.

It's my second summer season working in the Alps as an International Mountain Leader. Life has changed so much that I'm now spending more and more time at our little apartment at the foot of Mont Blanc, a new home in a favourite place. I've just led back-to-back to back trips with clients—nearly six weeks on the trail—but now I've got a week to myself. Originally the plan had been that a friend would fly out and we'd tick off some more of the 4,000ers, but he's still got a 'proper' job and suddenly can't make it over. I'm at a loose end. Even a year ago this would have been an unseen panic. I probably wouldn't have been aware enough to recognise it as such, but anxiety would wake the black dog and goad him to take charge and almost unawares I'd find myself making plans, getting myself to one of the bars in Chamonix where the Brit climbers hang out, reading guidebooks to work out just what I could solo, what would fill my time. That me, the only now sometimes me, that me would be looking for a way to escape already.

I wake from a really deep slumber. The little apartment has shutters and when they're closed it's impossible to tell if it's night or day; I open them to brilliant sun and the sort of warmth that tells you it's late already. I groggily wander into the lounge, which is also the kitchen and the dining room and the occasional office and put on the espresso pot. Its hissing wakes me again and cup in hand I head out onto the balcony and switch on my phone. Its 3pm! I've slept 15 hours, something simply unheard of. I'm surprised, but I'm still drinking a lot and adding in pain meds now and then, so I shrug it off. With the cupboards empty I decide to wander into town.

It's easy to buy another large coffee in the square and find a bench to sit and look out across the gorge—St Gervais les Bains really is the most beautiful village, made even better by its spectacular location—in every direction it is ringed by different mountain ranges; the Aravis, the Warrens and the Fiz are all prominent, whilst to the south Mont Blanc stretches ever upwards above all else. I sit a while and look at these hills I can see from our second home and feel something so long gone that I can't yet recall its name. My hands tingle with the desire to climb some of these unknown peaks simply because I see them so often and feel a yearning to know them more intimately. With a plan forming I amble homeward via the Guide's bar, practice my French a while, offer a few tips to some Brit holiday makers and buy some cheese for supper.

Now you may well recognise some of this behaviour—someone happily pottering around on a day off, maybe on holiday, enjoying a break, chilling out, making plans. I didn't then, it just wasn't something that happened. The me sat in the square with a coffee is four-and-a-half decades old and simply doesn't know how to rest and relax, has spent far too long far too tense and angry, carrying far too much internal weight.

The next morning I open the shutters seemingly ahead of the alarm, and again the warmth contradicts my assumption. In fact I've slept through the alarm, it's mid-morning. I'm annoyed at myself, the packed rucksack by the door mocks me, the day is wasted, I'm more than disappointed.

I'm a coffee person. The second one sees me sat on the balcony. From here I can see my objective for the day – the Pointe d'Anterne. sharp and dominant it looks down at me and laughs. I knew I needed an early start. I knew I wanted to climb the first cliffs before the sun got high… and yet I've slept in like a fat middle-aged holidaymaker. The third coffee jolts me into a mood of doing, and without much of a plan I'm in the van and driving through the village. The rucksack is packed for the planned but now lost day ahead in the Désert de Platé and without any discernibly conscious thought that's where I head. By the time I'm parked I've decided I'll just go for a wander to see what I can see. I stomp off without much good grace, glad to be alone.

But something as simple as movement feels noticeably great —I'm well rested, strong, there's a literal bounce in my step and it is a gloriously good day. My route starts on the ski slopes of this little resort, forty minutes steeply uphill, and it's heavenly. Enough exertion to feel in my legs, but no clients to slow me, able to push on at my own pace. When I level out at the little forest track I'm drenched in sweat but grinning from ear to ear – I soak myself in the alpine water trough and head into the shade of the high trees. Everywhere nature is abundant in its glory. I know the names of far more of the wildflowers I see here than I do of those back in the UK, it seems like I see more butterflies in an hour that I do in a year on our cold little island. I take pictures of all the ones I don't know so I can spend the evening identifying them. I'm engrossed in the world.

Around the high summer settlement of Ayéres des Rocs the massive cliffs of the Rochers des Fiz rise vertically into the sky, their simple geology meaning the trees disappear and the landscape changes dramatically. This panorama has fascinated me for the last five years. Easily overlooked next to the Mont Blanc range – these precipitous bastions are quite literally awesome. Even with binoculars they look impenetrable, their scale magnifying their sense of fortitude. Yet I know there are two easy breaches of these cliffs that give access to their secrets, a route towards their lofty sentinels. Without any further thought I take the faint rising trail. Even here as I climb into a spectacular landscape shaped by the rocks colour can be seen everywhere: the rich blues of the gentians, rare orchids in yellows, whites and reds, it's a glorious place to be. Alone in my element I'm moving fast in the glare of the early afternoon sun, but I'm glad to pause in the cool of a high snow patch which has survived in the perpetual shade of a huge fin of rock. I sit with my back to the cold wall and realise I can see my breath. For a while I'm fascinated by this visual representation of my work rate—I focus on slowing and deepening my breaths—an echo of future mindful moments that will connect another me to his own version of now. Rested, I push on.

As ever with this much scale to contend with the way only becomes apparent as I gain height. Features invisible from below become obvious and now le Dérochoir, the break that takes me into the Désert, comes into view—a line of metal staples hammered into the rock glint in a way that entices far too much and makes ignoring them impossible. Another hundred metres of height and I crest the most spectacular ridge into another landscape. Behind me, a mile lower down in the valley man holds dominion: water harnessed for hydroelectricity, the defence of the high passes breached with an implausible vaulting viaduct and eventually even the mass of the mightiest mountain defiled with the tunnel to Italy.

But. Everything in this moment is about where I'm stood, the different world I've entered.

Geology drawn across the land in the most grandiose of designs, the summits needle sharp, pointed in their prominence, daring you to challenge them. A high karst plateau where the limestone appears to flow as if poured by playful gods. And looking across at me from his high ledge on the cliff a majestic male bouquetin hardly registers my insignificance in this, his kingdom.

Far off to the right lies my original plan, but every direction offers other equally appealing alternatives.

I sit with a warm drink on a warmer rock, the air here noticeably cooler, the sun slowly starting to fall. I feel a sensation it will take me more years yet to recognise and longer still to learn the wisdom of seeking or the value of accepting.

I feel peace.

Only the hindsighted wisdom that the construction of these words has afforded the future me in writing this recollection lets me now appreciate that this was the moment. I've searched through the memory of all of those hard days in the mountains prior to then and, whilst I've surely felt its hinted presence before in other hopeful flashes, when I relax all of me into finding the moment of the revelation of that inner tranquillity again it is to this point in time my mind goes first. I can find it often sat wherever half a life later; but any definitive sense of peace before then is hard to see.

I sit atop the cooling cliff and look back at where I've made my way from.

It's a mindful metaphor made manifest—the climb taking me away from the stressful busy places of man, my apartment, even the village impossible to see. Back through the simpler life of the high alpine village and then gracefully into the wilds of nature. My attention moved from the complexities of machinery and nuances of language to the simplicity of existence to the beauty and wonderous immensity of the natural world. I've left my annoyance, anger and anxieties behind, not just forgotten, but rather not with me at all.

At first I thought I was simply tired, I'd taken on too much in the heat of the day. But as I sat there and let my senses check through my body I knew I felt invigorated. I knew I could push on, go further, but it wasn't that I couldn't be bothered or didn't care, all reasons that had stopped me on dark days in the past, it was something that felt simply more. I felt content with where I was, and, for the first time in too long, with what I was. I felt wholly alive—awoken inside, connected once again.

I can only wrap this in mediative words later learned; at the time, I simply sat and was.

At peace. I realised that I'd felt not a hint of the black dog's presence, heard not a single one of my shades whispering in the back of my mind, there'd been no shadow of the abyss that often held me.

By this point in my journey I'd become adept at more radical ways of reaching a similar state, I could quieten the voices high on a cliff, I could fall deep to sleep simply shattered from 18 hours dealing with clients. But both took a toll I was neither wise enough to fear or aware enough to acknowledge.

But this was something else, something different to my recent norm. I felt calm; internal quiet. Peace.

No part of the day had been especially difficult, certainly not dangerous. I could remember hanging off a ladder on the last cliff, leaning far out to watch a female ibex and her infant make their way gracefully along an inches—wide ledge on the face. I knew my phone was full of dozens of pictures of potentially rare, new-to-me wildflowers. I laughed out loud remembering the odd little beetle I'd found that nature had disguised as a bee.

I sat and pondered. I'd not been avoiding thoughts of Mum, I was no longer either disappointed at myself or angry that I wasn't heading higher. The process of thinking about it also looped round on itself and I noticed that I wasn't finding thinking about this difficult, I was conscious I wasn't distracting myself. More—I noticeably couldn't feel the weight I almost always knew was there. I wasn't avoiding the darkness because today I wasn't carrying it with me.

Curious, I pushed my mind towards asking myself tougher questions, questions I knew didn't usually have good answers—how I felt about not heading for a summit? Had I let myself down? Was this really the me I was supposed to be becoming? Was this yet another failure? And in the middle of doing so I heard myself laugh my mother's familiar laugh. "Enough" said a quiet inner voice, "this is more than enough for now".

I've so often used my time spent in the mountains to try and push myself past, to force myself through, to burn into being a different reality if only for a transient moment of respite. So often I've found that it's here more than anywhere else that I feel closest to finding an answer, it's here that I think I'll find my own truth and yet somehow, even in the burning bright, it's eluded me.

I'm sat on a rock somewhere in the high mountains, where or why no longer important. I've pushed myself as hard as ever to be here, I can feel my heart hammering, my breath ragged, but I also feel unburdened, free, able to think clearly, able to ask myself questions I've done everything to avoid. Finally I'm knowing this truth for myself: it's always better to ask these questions in peace rather than with anger.

For so long how we lost Mum threatened to overshadow everything else. But finally I'm coming to realise that in always pushing to find an understanding I've not seen the truth of what matters most in these words I've said so often: "we lost Mum". The how was horrific, but it's not having her here with us that really matters. If I can let go of the how and know that I carry her on in my heart then perhaps that's the start of something better.

I'm high on the Cairngorm plateau—I thought I could race the weather, but whilst I'm still learning just what the ankle is capable of now that I can finally walk again, I've not yet realised how heavy the pain that remains is going to be. Though I may not still have a shard of bone drilling its way through the joint, repairing that has destroyed several small ligaments, I've no longer any cartilage and the nerves are always inflamed and waiting to scream. The leverage generated with inch high crampon points trying to bite into occasional patches of bullet hard ice on top of jagged rocks only serves to magnify everything tenfold. Behind me the sun is dropping incredibly fast into the mountains of the west, my own long shadow tells me without needing to look that soon it will be dark.

I'd set out early, a fantastically crisp day, too good to waste. Even tired from weeks in the hills already I knew I had to go. Scotland on a day like this is as good as it gets.

The climb out of the Lairig Ghru had been far more difficult than I'd anticipated. By the time I'd realised just how hard the ice was, how delicately I was going to have to climb 300ft on the points of crampons and axes I was already past the sort of ground I didn't want to retreat over. Up to the relative safety of the plateau, up into the gullies seemed far quicker and safer. And whilst it was difficult, I was in my element. I'd mastered relaxing into the repetitive rhythm of steadily moving upwards, I was focused. But the exertion and all those prior days were taking a toll, I could feel myself tiring, the axes becoming hard to hold.

As I neared the finish of the climb I'd have been forgiven for thinking there were other climbers ahead of me, I knew what this much icy shrapnel scathing down on me meant. In a little fork of a gully just before the top I stopped and dug a small ledge—time for a hot drink, food and dry gloves. Everything clipped to an axe wedged in the protruding fingers of rock, sunglasses swapped for goggles.

This would be a good place to meet your end, to say your goodbyes and set forth on the next great adventure.

But not today.

Adrenalin and dopamine still flood my system, I'm feeling good, but I know what the wild-blown snow above me means; the fun stuff is over, now I've got to make it home. I hate this navigation thing, but that's why I do it. Climbing has just been escapism, avoidance. I make a plan. Navigationally I know the plateau can be a graveyard; on the wrong day, on many a wrong day, this is the very worst place to be lost in the UK. I pack my stuff—this stop has been less than five minutes and already I can feel the frost forming on my bones. I loosen my boots and with my head down against the sharp wind I make my way out of the gully and up onto the broad flanks of Cairn Lochan.

The going is immensely tough. The snow crust only holding my weight for every second, fourth, fifth, tenth random step – when I break through its thigh deep, each step is exhausting. And the shrill pain in my ankle is starting to sing the siren's song of despair and loss.

Adjust the plan. Change the goal. I don't want to.

Accept the pain. The pain that's stopped me on so many days, the pain that hints at so much worse.

Accept the pain. Give thanks for it. The pain means I'm here. I could surrender and simply sit at a desk and it might never hurt again. But.

The pain is because I'm doing one of the many things I thought I'd never do again.

The pain is just a reminder to be grateful for what I can do. It's not the whole of me anymore however much it hurts, however much it reminds me of the fear of what was so nearly lost, however much the dark wants to tell me I deserve it.

Thigh deep in snow again I hear a strange, muffled sound. I'm laughing. Undeniably this is fun. Admittedly that strange 'type two' fun that those who play in the great outdoors relish so much, but fun all the same. I cast a glance back: my deep, shadowed tracks make an almost straight line to the setting sun. Truth be told I'm a little surprised by both how far I've come and how little progress I seem to have made. But this isn't the place or time for metaphorically metaphysical wordplay.

The biting wind has dropped. Head down, working physically hard, I haven't noticed. With the right equipment and clothing I've not been worried by it, simply hindered. But now it's appreciably less, something I've noticed happens often as the rise and fall of the sun heralds the beginning and end of the day, a strangely magical window of calm. Looking back as the sky turns the burnished gold of wonder I can see the flow of the wind as it weaves the snow in beautifully sinuous patterns across the plateau. It's a moment to savour and simply be.

I dig a seat into the snow using what I move to build a low wall to shelter me from the snow snakes, laughing at my old creakiness I dig a deeper hole for my feet so I don't have to bend my knees too much. A lukewarm drink and a homemade flapjack. I sit and I breathe in the scene before me. Already the snow is filling my tracks, which now seem to magically appear halfway along my journey, it only adds to the specialness of having all this to myself. But I'm not alone, not anymore. I've learned in these moments not just to give thanks for the majesty before me, but also to give thanks for my place within it, to give thanks for those who helped me, who've supported me, who've lifted me up to here. Appreciation of being able to be in this place right now. The gratitude that if I can do this for today at least then that is something worth celebration. I know that even recently there'd have been an inconsolable sadness within me that I'll never be able to show this view to my mum and that would have so quickly connected to the reason why; but now I'm coming to understand that she'd only have really seen this through me, through my words, my experience, my telling. I now know that if I hold her in my heart then she can still see it through my eyes, she can still feel it in my gratitude for the life she gave me, the strength I now have.

I could dig in and just wait this out, maybe see the dawn, I've the kit to survive a night here. I could get up and get moving, force myself to be quicker. But I don't do either; simply being here now and experiencing every aspect of it is the most important thing. Feed the soul, revive and replenish the body. Watch the ice crystals dance as the wind builds and drops. All of creation and yet only me is seeing this now. I know I could (maybe should) move fast from here and be off the hill in the gloaming, but I also know moments as special as this are a blessing to be accepted, a gift to appreciate fully. I can feel the summit's presence behind me, I know from there it's a simple walk down. I sit and absorb as much of the wonder as I can while the light fades; I want to be able to share this with the people I love.

A different meditation, one just as strong.

Not what you wanted, more than you could hope for.

The day I wander into the wonder, words written almost last that tell so much of before, possibly all of what's next.

There's a quiet beauty in the hills where I live. I've said for so long that it had taken me half a lifetime to learn to appreciate these hills I see most often. One of the little truths learned along the way: it took a decade of fire to remember to see the wonder in everything. These gentle hills have always been beautiful.

When I wander here now I see that beauty magnified by the love I have for what here means, the love I have for those I've shared here with, the love I have for those not yet met that I want to bring here. To walk here is to forever walk with a beautiful white dog and hear her sing the song of her kind when the wind blows wild—to play with a bouncing puppy and fathom the love they'd have had for each other, to appreciate the place I share in that.

I wander often to a favourite place, the lonely larch atop the Knott. Not just shaped by its environment but defined by it, standing solitary and strong, defiantly definitely of it. I sit here often and feel much the same. It's a place to pause and delight in the play of light as clouds shadow Wainwright's 'sleeping elephants', the ancient Howgills, the quiet giants at the heart of here.

Some of the last words of remembrance; April 9th 2020.

I knew I could have broken lockdown, I oh-so-nearly did, in the early hours whilst the world slept on. I nearly ignored all else in a quest to take what I felt should be mine. There's now no version of me that would have called a team to peril if anything went wrong, I'd never put anyone at risk, but equally I'd never want the people I love to have those hours of worry. And I know now. Be your best you when you can. Even if it isn't your always you.

In the last couple of years this day has been a physical struggle, a celebration so nearly lost. But still I've craved the challenge, needed to push myself again, felt a yearning for the edge, even if I've felt far from its meaning, perhaps lost to its truth. But ever and always, a but; this year, with Mum a decade gone and me a decade different that's not the me stood here on this day. Maybe tomorrow, certainly many a yesteryear, but not this today, not for now.

Today with the high places put out of reach by the pandemic I was thankful I'm now aware enough to know what the truth of this day really is, what it really means. Today I decided to show Mum my place in this world, a long looping wander of where we now live, somewhere she never got to visit. This is the place I've lived longest in my entire life, the first place a little lost boy has called home. It seems right to show someone I love where I love.

Me, my mum and Missy walked out of the hole in the wall and made our way up onto the high fell and past the lonely larch. We paused and gave thanks that, as every year has been, this special day was simply stunning again. We smiled in remembrance of a beautiful white dog's song often heard in this her favourite haunt. Then with the warm sun on my back and that song echoing in my heart we wandered out onto the shining stones. We made a wiggled way, hopping across grikes from clint to clint, physically stronger than in a long time, calmer than in, well, a decade. Missy's exuberance is the hope of tomorrow made magically real.

But today is the day I make my reckoning, try to fathom a peace, maybe something, anything, more.

So many of these days have involved so much risk in search of a reward of the empty, yet so few of those risks took me any closer to balancing the scales of my life. Whilst they briefly burned bright they ultimately left me still in the dark.

Today is the day I make my reckoning but I'm not alone. I sit a while in this favourite place and I think of all those I love. Am I trying to be my best for them? Am I doing everything I can to make now and tomorrow better than yesterday? Am I finally getting an understanding of what the journey should be all about?

I know I'll never find all of my answers—but who ever does? I know I'll always yearn for an impossible, have a longing for what's lost, but I can now find a peace with that. This decade of torment has seen so many inconsequential things forever lost to time, things that once seemed unassailable in their import fade away to nothing. That I now see love as a joy rather than a sorrow seems simply right.

Walking in the wonder with Mum today I heard her laugh again, I felt her love lift me, make me stronger and I smiled a lot in the remembering.

I spent so long trying to avoid looking at it. So long hoping it would disappear in the distraction of doing or somehow fade away if I pushed myself hard enough. For a while it seemed I could simply shout louder than the whispering voices, I could make my bark worse than that of the black dog, that risk would lead to reward. But the monsters of the darklands are used to waiting, their plan is always to wear you down with their relentlessness. Eventually you must bring them out into the light and see them for what they really are.

Out in the light on the good days, the days when I feel strong enough, I became able to talk about them with others, to think clearly and logically about them in a totality rather than gruesome abstraction, and slowly, imperceptibly they got less. Had I gotten stronger?

There were flashes in the high mountains—the unbidden laugh that arose unconsciously, the creativity and focus that often followed excess—but they were ephemeral, impossible to hold on to, decorative parapets on a self with weak foundations, something I couldn't summon at will, that felt not quite all of me.

Which leads me in a future moment of nowful wisdom to the question; Was it the endeavour, the place or the pause that mattered most?

I tried the endeavour for so very long, did my very best to burn bright in the doing of deeds. And it would be truly churlish to suggest there wasn't a goodly measure of betterment in building a sense of self on something other than loss, that the respite gained almost certainly made one of the cracks that let the light in.

My inclination and opportunity for place to so often be spectacular most definitely let me remember how to find the ways to appreciate the now, to shift my focus from my inner darkness to the wonderment often found in the world.

But. It was the pause, the moments of acknowledging, the slowly finding the strength to start a conversation, even if only with myself at first—that was when healing began to be a thing. Knowing I could be at peace stood still, simply happy with existing, not running or fighting—that was when I started to find a real sense that there might be a path out into the future that was also a path back to loving life.

I could have walked all the miles of a Muggle's lifetime and never known. Alone and disconnected high in the mountains avoiding others I was absent from so much, I had no appreciation of the true worth of what remained, that which could still be lost. It was only when I paused and let the peace grow in me that I began to understand the value of what still to come.

A wiser man than me might have known that this was the path to acceptance.

Chapter 10

Acceptance; Resting in peace

How do you make a peace from the broken pieces of a life? How do you find a way to accept the unacceptable?

That the life I now live and love is a direct consequence of Mum being murdered is inescapable. It's determinedly determinist in the progression from there to here even if the path has been winding and lost to sight for many a moment. When Mum was killed everything changed. On many levels it often feels fundamentally wrong that some of that change was undeniably for the better. Without her loss I would probably still be floundering and flabby in a life I really wasn't enjoying anymore, simply surviving, nowhere near to thriving. My return to the mountains, the slowly salvaged sense of self, this internal peace I've finally found, they'd all be things unknowingly no more, an alternate reality not realised. Whilst I may never have fallen, would I have remembered what it is to fly?

But, ever and always, this is the *but* that puts a pause in my step, the tainted truth that twists the knife in the dark: I'd still have a mum.

Learning to accept the contrast within that terrible circumstance has probably been the last lesson to learn on the long road back to loving life. It's also been the hardest.

I've said before I'd make that deal with a God I no longer know. But of course, there's no deal to be made, the real world doesn't work that way however much you wish it would. A soul may well be the most valuable thing we each possess, but it turns out you can't sell it even when there's a version of you forever stood at those metaphorical crossroads hoping to find salvation in the impossible.

Reality rules with a hard, heavy hand in the really real world of the here and now.

So many hypothetical alternative variations of me vie for attention in the dark. Would I, could I, why didn't I all echo in the deep of the abyss, impossible questions knowing the damage they're asking causes. Would I have done the right thing? Would I have done a wrong right thing? Could I have hurt him enough? Should I have loved her more? Would his abuse of her have continued unseen whatever I did? Could we ever have had that conversation? Would I have returned to the mountains? Would I ever have done something about living unhappily without that bitter red pill? Would I still end up physically broken? Should I always deserve to be in pain because I let her be taken? The process of asking, the futility of wishing, a viciously visceral self-harm; guilt's last grasp attempt to hold you fast in the past.

In those long hours of the night, during the many days spent lost in the dark, then it's all too easy for blame and doubt to overwhelm. It's the easiest thing in the world for being happy to seem like the very worst thing in the world. When you begin to hate yourself it becomes easy to believe you deserve to hurt. If you hate yourself it becomes easier to hurt yourself. When you no longer love yourself it's easy to fall into believing no one could or should love you anymore, again or ever. And when you no longer love yourself it's easy to stop loving what really matters.

How do you reconcile that something as good as now could ever emerge from something as evil as that one dreadful moment in time?

Travelling back and forth through the last past decade of scribbled words, notes and thoughts I don't even mention the concept of acceptance until this most recent year of finding my way out of the dark. Until I'm a long way out into the light, until the bad days are few and far between. It turns out people far wiser than at least me might have gotten the understanding of this process right. Acceptance comes last, as perhaps it must.

With its dawning comes a revelatory realisation: one more moment of self-awareness, maybe a hard new lesson learned or perhaps another lost truth found again as the hate-fuelled fire inside finally flickers and fades. There's so much more to accept than the loss of Mum and the manner in which she was taken from us. The journey of this last decade has illuminated so much of the years before, it's forced me to re-evaluate the opportunity of those still to come and challenged my own beliefs of what was and what might be. I've spent the last parts of this process finding the way to accept the meaning of so many other memories and moments glimpsed through the lens of the hole in my heart. I suspect a psychoanalyst would have a small chuckle, a Jungian stroke of the chin at my subconscious word foolery, because acceptance, acceptance at the end of it all, at the start of everything after, acceptance is about making your heart whole again.

I fought for so long to not become definitively the son of a murdered mum; I strived just as long to be the something other I thought I'd find an escapist salvation in, her son the mountaineer, and in the doing of each I lost sight of the rest of who I was, who I could be, who I should be. I never even noticed till it was done that both those prescriptive descriptives shared one word that should have meant more than all the others.

I forgot for so long that the greatest gift of life is choice.

I ran through an alphabet of alternatives doing all I could to avoid the consideration that acceptance should or could ever be a possibility. For so long the very concept of acceptance was simply unacceptable. Avoiding, burying, castigating, deceiving, escaping, fighting, gone—all seemed the most likely outcome, finding ways to force my focus elsewhere seemed the best I could ever hope to achieve. Succumbing to acceptance seemed a fallow weakness. Foolish to the end, I'd no idea how much strength it would both take and give. The climber in me, the defiant little boy, the vengeful grown man, so many versions of me—they all screamed inside to hold on, to keep the angry fire alive. It took the longest time to acknowledge the quiet counsel of my ghosts that knew I had to let go.

And it's not as simple as a decision or a destination; it's the very purpose of the journey. I can't tell you your secret because that's not how magic works, you have to find your own way to believe. Like all the best magic tricks it surprised me just as much as anyone else. Just when I thought the hope of it was lost in any real sense, so near to both the end and a new beginning, faith found it for me. And no, I've not made my peace with some sadly still lacking deity, but I have found the wonder in the world again. I've hinted at it, glimpsed it from afar, wrapped it in different words, danced myself all around an understanding of it, lost to the truth that it was there all along. People are the very real wonder in the world, people are the source of the love in the world. I've told you I know that love saved me, and that's the faith I finally found. Scattered through the words of a decade and the memories of a lifetime that's the golden thread that kept me tethered to today, the lifeline that pulled me back into the light. People who mattered to me, those seemingly gone, those still by my side, those ever present. People I didn't acknowledge then but give thanks for now, people long not seen who I know I should thank evermore, and most amazingly people I've yet to meet who I believe will come to mean so much.

And yet acceptance, even wrapped in all the love I thought I knew, that was always something never to be deserved, impossible, that asked too much to ever consider. Until it wasn't. Until it just was. That's how magic works.

I could, should, might, tell you about positive reinforcement, I might even call it belief. Love gives you the capacity for that. Developing the belief you can fly, having the emotional resilience to lift yourself up, to turn your eyes from the dark, even just the hope of love, they all reinforce a sense of a worthwhile self, a sense of believing in tomorrow being better. And still it takes more, it doesn't just happen from the passing of time or the quietening of a soul: it builds incrementally until it just is. There was never an awareness, for me, of moving towards it or arriving. One day I just knew I could look into the dark and the stars would be the most important thing I saw.

Acceptance didn't come when I accepted I was loved; somewhere a part of me has always known my nearest and dearest loved me. It didn't even come when I started to put more love out into the world; I hope they've always known I love them. Its seed sprouted unseen when I began to believe again that I really was worth loving for who I am now, that I'm the sum of more than just my past actions or lack thereof. I'm the sum of my hopes, aspirations, failures, successes. It grows when you understand that whilst it's a part of you that you'll always carry you are not defined by the dark, your failures are not the all of you or even the most of you. You are so much more than that, you are the sum of all that magnified by all the love ever placed in you. And I know, believe me. I really know.

If you're lost in the dark, if life has knocked you down for now then you're probably sat there reading this and you're saying to yourself that no one loves you, no one could ever love you. You'll say that she, he, they are gone, maybe never were, maybe never will be. You'll maybe think there's nothing worth loving about you, that nobody cares, that everyone is better off without you.

But.

This one really matters—and yes, I know how impossible what I'm about to write will seem as you read it, I know I'd have ignored it for so long, I'd have hit it with everything I could to prove it wrong and I know you feel the same if you're held by the abyss. But still. This one really matters.

Out in the light I can look you in the eye and tell you this one true thing. However dark it is, however bad it seems, the world remains, and it's a thing full of love. And yes, you might even accept that's true, but if you're lost in the dark you'll believe it doesn't apply to you, that you don't deserve it to apply to you, that a world of love is for other people, not you.

So if you take nothing else from all these words take this:

I care about you and have love for you and I might not even know you yet.

It's a choice given freely. Everything else can be built on that. And I'm not alone or special when I tell you this—there's far more good than bad people in the world, there are an infinite number of stars shining in the dark. There are little old ladies who embrace broken strangers in the street, there are people who look you in the eye across a horrified courtroom and show they care with whispered words of compassion. There are the people who lift a fallen little boy up, the ones who shelter him from the storm. There are the strangers who pass you on your way and simply smile with a warm hello and the people answering phones in the middle of the night. There are people who choose to walk into the dark to find you, people who'll sit in that dark with you just so you know you're not alone. There are so many people who care. There's a world of love out there waiting for you.

Each time I venture out into the mountains I now know I carry Mum, and all the other loves I've had and have in my life with me. Heading out into the wilderness, making my own way in the mountains, this was where I slowly relearned the truth of that as I felt their strength lift me. Walking into the wonder and finding the places to pause and ponder both within and without, that was the when of the words taking shape, the start of understanding how I might begin to find my own way again. Slowly as I reconnected with the natural world and let the sense of peace that nature always brings calm my internal noise so I began to connect with others, talk with others, let them see and know all of me. Finally I became able to connect with my ghosts, came to really appreciate the importance of why I carry them with me, how I can best honour them moving forward. As I came to understand that coming back from adventures, coming home, a word I so seldom used to use, coming home better than I left, coming home glad to return, each time a little closer – as I came to recognise the importance of that I think acceptance began to become an unseen possibility. It's a fool's errand to try and measure the incremental steps on the longest and hardest walks. Often your head is down, sometimes you're just fighting to survive, sometimes you might be struggling to keep pace, focused fully in the now, possibly dragging the impossible weight of the past. So often the distance you've physically travelled is the least important part of the journey. And then there's a moment. You look up and realise how far you've come, how much has changed.

I know the high wild places will always be my personal cathedral, the place I feel closest to my happiest version of me, but they're not now the only place that I can be my best version of me. Being in the mountains will always mean so much to me on a personal level—but in spending so long searching out only those high places, in casting my eyes ever upwards I missed out on another of the great truths. The real magic is everywhere.

In finally coming to understand and find an acceptance of the how, what and why of my life I've learned that I don't need to push myself right to the edge to find my inner peace. I don't need to risk losing it to value the love I have. For so long the peace I went looking for, the peace I thought I found, it was actually just the absence of the bad I couldn't deny rather than any acceptance of the good I'd lost my appreciation of. I spent far too long trying to empty myself when what I really needed, what all of us need, is to be full and whole. Wholly ourselves, fully present.

I never really spent any time in denial and I was never delusional, I always accepted the physical fact Mum was gone. The same logic, however painful to contemplate, applied to the manner of her going. That was never the acceptance I struggled to acknowledge. Knowing I didn't do the right thing, knowing my version of the right thing would have been wrong, knowing I didn't do anything, I thought I'd hate myself forever for my complicity in how we lost her and I was ready to accept that was the fate I deserved. When I reached the depths of my depression I started to believe that I wasn't worth the love this life has to offer, I found it impossible to accept that any good should come from such a tragedy.

In striving so hard to remake myself a new version of an old forgotten dream, in pushing myself to try to accomplish achievements I thought Mum or maybe I could be proud of I slowly began to understand something that you, my lone reader, may well already know. I'd hope it's a lesson most learn young, but it's been a revelation to me. I know it is to many of us who've wandered lost in the dark.

It was never what I did that mattered.

It was never even how I did it. Looking back would my mum really have been able to name more than a couple of mountains — would she have understood that famous Mont Blanc was a walk? That the never-heard-of before Lyskamm paralysed me with fear? Would anyone outside of climbing's insular little world ever really care about the nuanced equations of E5 6a versus E4 6b? Know how all-consuming adding that + to a climb could be? I've slowly come to comprehend that was never what it was about. Those fleetingly futile achievements weren't the reason she smiled then or now. She was smiling because she was finally seeing her son fly. She smiled in the glow of knowing she'd raised more than a survivor, her smile was the joy of seeing a life lived well, seeing happiness bloom into being. It was what every mother wants for her child. They want to shelter them from the dark, they want them to thrive in the light.

When I wander in the wonder now, whether alone, with loved ones or clients, there are often magical moments when appreciation simply makes me stop and then I know, really know. I'll pause and wait for her smile to cross my face or to hear her laughter on the wind—and it's then that I know I'm living my best life, being my best me, honouring Mum, and deserving the love I've found in the world.

It's not been a part of the journey I ever gave any thought. I really never saw an outcome where guilt and self-recrimination weren't a part of the deal; the best I hoped for was a future where I found a way to carry the weight, to not be broken by it. I lived with pain for so long that it seemed an acceptable price to pay, a fair reward for failure—that was as close to acceptance as I thought I'd ever get. Love had other ideas.

It's January 2020, Mum a decade gone, me a decade different. I've walked out of the white room feeling brilliantly alive. It's the first time I write the word *acceptance* in my journal in any sort of positive way. A decade. I've written before about Ms Kubler-Ross, I've been scornful, I've been cynical, I thought it was another of those things that no longer applied to me. I'm starting to have an inkling I may well owe her an apology.

I'm sat in a court room as the verdict is read out, it's July 2010. I can taste the rust iron sharp in my blood as I clench my teeth to keep me in my seat. I'm burning with something far out there beyond anger, the internal fire forge hot, to sear into being a resolve I can't yet escape. I want to hold all of this pain in a strong little box until I'm alone in the dark with him and I can pay it back tenfold. Acceptance isn't any of the options in my mind. I'm going to have to wait 23 years to exact a retribution I think I can accept.

My fingers scream as I pull on the smallest of edges. It's June 2015 and my weight tips into balance as I rock over on Froggatt's great slab, the boulders below beckon the ghost of old and future consequence. I'm not sure I can or should do this anymore. I've accepted falling will hurt. I still deserve to hurt.

April 9th 2021

And yet walking in the high wild places with Mum today I heard her laugh and felt her love within me, I felt it making me stronger and I smiled in the moments of realisation.

For today at least I can accept that.

I went looking for the love in the world again and slowly and gently it worked its magic on me, brought me back to life. Tentatively I began to try and coax my own love out and into being. I didn't notice that slowly the journey had come to matter more, I didn't realise that the destination had changed, it wasn't something I was conscious of. Perhaps for once I wasn't listening to those infernal internal voices whispering in the recesses of my mind. I wandered out into the wonder; I spent time slowly opening myself up to the good in the world and bit by imperceptible bit slowly I changed. I grew, I relaxed, I let go and I gave unto others. Quietly, with no fanfare at all, acceptance came and found me.

I've often said that I believe scars can only heal when they're exposed to the light—and I've become the proof of that now. For so long life taught me to lock things away in strong little boxes and hide them away. Another contradiction: we learn early on not to have the difficult conversations, we're told time and again that people don't really want to know how you are, the question is but a conversational pause in a stride: walk on, nothing to see here. Often our pixellated version of friends are all about the image, so long as it's a happy one is the oft quoted new wisdom. People, we're socially taught to believe, don't want to see scars.

But as I walked further out into the light and falteringly began to let go these words, started to show people my scars, stopped to acknowledge the bravery in theirs, ever so slowly I discovered a far more wonderful way of seeing the world, just forgotten for some, a lesson missed for others, an old truth lost to me for too long.

People are the good in the world.

Bit by bit I let the words slip out and into being. We're so often told to put a brave smile on it, people don't want to hear your sorrows. A trouble shared is a friend lost. And it's simply not true. I've sat on a rock in the high mountains not able to make eye contact and told people the very worst of me, and they've not recoiled, they've not made excuses and left. I've been hugged, held hard and helped. I've been shown so many times the capacity people have to be more than we imagine, better than we're told to believe.

I've made more true friends in this latter life than in all the decades before. I've fallen deeper in love with old friends than I thought possible. I've passed people and noticed the smiling faces, assumed the best of them, not the worst. People are the good in the world. The me lost in the dark couldn't see it—but the simple truth is that people guided me into the light. There were few heroics on my part. Maybe I can claim the strength and resilience to have looked up, maybe I remembered enough to look out rather than in. But people, more people than I ever thought possible, people filled with love and goodness saved me, even if so many of them will never know or realise the worth of what they did.

Talking therapy—finding your own voice. Learning to listen for the truths that awaken in the moments of silence. Having the strength to sing your own song. Defining yourself with your own words, believing the good people say about you. Telling people for the first time. Not flinching from others. Taking the offered hand. All steps towards acceptance.

Slowly I let go. It doesn't come easy. Perhaps it shouldn't. I don't want to fall again. On the good days, and they're mostly all good now, I know I can fly. But. I don't want to fall again. I didn't think living in fear of a thing had been my thing since the day I left home leaving the life I was fearful of behind. Yet fear is insidious, it hides in the cracks, it bides its time. Much as the simple act of water freezing can reduce a mountain range to rubble, fear breaks you down in many an unseen way too. Fear is often what keeps you holding on, but oh-so-often it stops you moving on. And it grows best in the dark.

Yet fear itself isn't a bad thing. It can be a good thing—fear can keep you alive. I've not climbed with many climbers who've had a real fear of heights but I do instinctively know I don't want to tie on with anyone who has no concept of fear. If we can't acknowledge it then why bother with all the safe simple systems? Why not just roll the dice? Sure I'll walk over to appreciate the view, but only a fool does pirouettes there. Those aren't the people you want to walk into the storm with. But you? You're a little apprehensive? You can acknowledge the fear you carry? Yes I'll walk with you. I know it can be scary, but I know it will be easier together—our sum is always more than our parts. And if it gets too much for a moment? Then we can sit in the grace of the world and reconnect, we'll let it imbue us, we'll each share our strength but we'll both move on stronger, there's less to be afraid of if we're together. Fear is just a tiny part of the whole, it's misprocessed information, it tells us there's something to be afraid of losing, that there's something that matters more, and when we learn to focus on that then the fear becomes simply the shadow that gives definition to what matters more.

It's one of those truisms I've tried so hard to avoid—but once you embrace and take ownership of your fear then it can no longer control you; I can't put it any better than that.

Life lessons learned slowly. I'll never be able to change what I didn't do. That scar on my soul was for so long a crack that let the darkness in, a gateway to where I thought I deserved to be.

But. The greatest gift of life is choice.

I'll never be able to change what I didn't do. But I can change what I take from that, change what I'll do not just in the tomorrows to come, but today, now, in this moment. I can now look at my scars and instead of seeing them as cruel reminders of past failures I can choose to see them as the foundations of future success. I'll never not have that conversation again. I'll never not let you know that I'm here for you, that I'll listen to you, love you, lend you my strength when you need it. Choices. My mum raised her son to know right from wrong.

I can choose to try and be the candle in someones dark and if I don't shine brightly enough then I promise I'll still sit there beside you. You don't have to be alone.

Accepting you didn't know. Accepting your answers were wrong. Accepting there is no wrong only learning, Accepting tomorrow is your choice. Accepting you are loved. Accepting you deserve to be loved.

Acceptance. I never knew I always knew.

Epilogue: Endings

As my journey to today gathered a momentum of its own, when these words first started to tumble forth, I imagined a grand plan that this long walk into the unknown to find an understanding of yesterday and tomorrow would finish with me stood atop a mighty peak, a rising sun casting long fortuitous shadows as I strode purposely on to the summit. And while every mountaineer and philosopher knows that reaching the top is only half the way to done, I still believed I needed to end on a high.

Yet even here, so many words into trying to find my answers, still, almost inevitably, there's a but.

Because as the words began to take shape I slowly came to understand that I wasn't looking for an ending, really I was trying to find a way to continue in grace. Wandering out into the wonder of it all I've come to realise that by searching for that ending I've rekindled a love of the journey. In looking so long into the abyss I've gained a deeper appreciation of the world around me.

For the longest time any and all thoughts of Mum were scarred by the intensity of how she was taken from us, the echoes of that loss threatening to eradicate all that had gone before, destroy any hope of what might follow. I came so close to letting love slip from my life, to letting my love of life itself be swallowed by the darkness. By the time I knew I was falling, I had already decided I deserved that fate and had forgotten what it meant to fly. I had almost forgotten that the world is filled with wonder and love.

And just when I thought I might be finding my way back to the light, I fell again. There were days dark with pain, months that stretched into years when I doubted I would ever walk in wild places again. The chance of me ever climbing more than the stairs seemed gone, and I began to be sure that was the ending I really deserved.

But so many people lifted me, encouraged me to go look for the good, reminded me that life truly does go on, that the world really is a place of infinite chances, helped me understand that forgiveness has to begin somewhere deep in yourself. Slowly, stumbling, step by step, I walked out of the dark guided by those shining stars, even if neither they nor I knew it at the time.

In doing so, I became another version of myself. The same person viewed differently. I learned to pause, to appreciate the wonder surrounding me, and to understand my place within it. Slowly, as nature calmed me and love lifted my gaze, hope began to take flight. In time, anger, regret, and self-recrimination softened. Self-forgiveness opened the door for acceptance, and I came to see just how much I still had to be grateful for. I finally remembered what it was to smile.

It's been a long decade but now I can look back past that fateful hole in time and remember happy moments when we were simply a son and his mum. These memories, though they once seemed few and far between, have become beacons of light. Some I've pieced together from photographs worn with age, others remain clear as the day they were made. All of them are vital to me now, each one a burning candle of love, lessening the dark and its shades of loss. These are some of the brightest stars guiding me into the future I now know I deserve—the future any mum would wish for her child.

Over this last decade I've had moments when I've considered my own ending. I think that is simply a part of the human condition. Thankfully though, even down in the darkest depths of depression and self-loathing I've never seriously considered ending my life. Even in the worst of my risk taking, in those moments when part of me knew my choices weren't anywhere close to my best, in the moments when I slunk away from the world, I just hoped it would hurt more than I already did, maybe burn bright enough to distract me from the abyss but, if not, then I deserved to feel what might be, deserved to be held by the fear of what was to come.

Yet now when I think of the idea of an ending I realise that I've had many lives that have ended before. I'm no longer the me that was quick to his fists, nor the beaten me down on the floor or the me wandering lost in the dark. I barely ever think of the incredibly tough decade building a business or the decade working for others and partying too hard. Those iterations of me seem fleetingly short in their actual import. Yet they are still a significant part of the me I am today. Slowly I've come to understand no part of us really ever ends or is lost. I've evolved, changed direction, found my own way in this the grandest journey of them all. And if this is true for me, it must also be true for those I love, those I've lost, and those who still live within me. Perhaps it's even true for you.

Over this past decade, I've experienced other losses too as all lives must. For a time, I wondered if Mum's loss would always overshadow everything, if nothing else could ever hurt as deeply. But while her death built my resilience, it also deepened my empathy and reminded me of the importance of giving and receiving. In coming to understand the impact Mum's loss had on me, and at the same time aware of how little impact it had or indeed should have had on strangers I've come to appreciate how unique each of us are, how none of us can ever assume what path another has taken to today or how hard their own journey might have been for them.

So near to the end of this telling, both in these words and the years of life, even closer in the moments of memory, balanced right here at the end of this version of now, other losses shine light into my life rather than deepening the darkness. They become future bright stars that show me more real truth than I ever found in the abyss. In the space of a few months I lost the nan that always sheltered me, the uncle that always made me laugh and the wonderful white dog who always walked by my side. I'm not ashamed to say each loss brought tears. Nan went to old age as well as any of us might hope, Uncle went before his time, making brave choices to the end and beautiful Pushka went because even the best of companions must reach the end of their own road. Each hurt as of course they should, but I smile a warm smile whenever I think of them now. Their love remains with me, a source of strength and light, joining the chorus of voices that guide me forwards in the wonder of it all. I'm more for their being not less because of their loss.

As my eyes have turned from then to tomorrow, I've come to understand the importance of now. I'll always carry my ghosts within me, it's their love that made me strong. But—yes even here, mere words from goodbye—but. The love I have now makes me stronger. The love I have of the world, the love I put back into it. The love I'm given, from family, friends old and new, the love I have for you, the love I know people not yet met have to offer.

All the best stories have a happy ending. But the truly great stories? Those are the ones that finish with a new beginning.

Life is the greatest story of them all.

Words of a new beginning to be read after all else

These words were largely pulled into existence as the world hid from a pandemic, as so many people's lives changed forever. I found the space to step back and look at the big picture. Slowly I began to see the why and how of the path from there to here.

In the midst of so much sorrow and loss I made an offer intended to put the words I'd written into practice—to take people out of themselves and into nature for a walk and a talk, to offer them a human connection, a chance to remember we're a social species, a safe and simple way to improve their mental and physical health.

And just like that, Wellness Walks was born: a way to offer back to the world a little of the love that's been given to me, to try and shine a light for those looking for a way to take the first steps towards feeling better.

Writing this it's 2025, we've just become a registered charity and we're building a community of fabulous leaders delivering Wellness Walks all across the UK. As a charity our mission is simple; we want as many people as possible, in as many places as possible, to be able to go on a totally free Wellness Walk.

The writing of this started as part of my own therapy, helped me see something, maybe someone, better. I never knew if it would ever be printed on to a page, let alone shared. But some of you read my drafts, encouraged me, said it should be a thing, might help that one other person find their way out of the dark. Any and all profits from this book will go to Wellness Walks to help make that mission a reality. So thank you, from me, from our Wellness Walkers and from the memory of my mum. She'd be smiling to read this.

With much love,

Kelvyn

wellnesswalks.org.uk

Find a Wellness Walk:

Donate to Wellness Walks:

Printed in Great Britain
by Amazon

61678469R00116